HEROES OF HISTORY

HARRIET TUBMAN

Freedombound

HEROES OF HISTORY

HARRIET TUBMAN

Freedombound

JANET & GEOFF BENGE

Emerald Books
P.O. BOX 635, LYNNWOOD, WA 98046

Emerald Books are distributed through YWAM Publishing. For a full list of titles, including other great biographies, visit our website at www.heroesofhistory.com or call 1-800-922-2143.

Harriet Tubman: Freedombound

Published by Emerald Books
P.O. Box 635
Lynnwood, WA 98046

ISBN 978-1-883002-90-9 (paperback)
ISBN 978-1-932096-72-9 (e-book)

Library of Congress Cataloging-in-Publication Data
Benge, Janet, 1958-
Harriet Tubman : freedombound / Janet and Geoff Benge.
p. cm. — (Heroes of history)
Includes bibliographical references (p.).
ISBN 1-883002-90-7
1. Tubman, Harriet, 1820?-1913—Juvenile literature. 2. Slaves—United States—Biography—Juvenile literature. 3. African American women—Biography—Juvenile literature. 4. Underground railroad—Juvenile literature. 5. Antislavery movements—United States—History—19th century—Juvenile literature. [1. Tubman, Harriet, 1820?-1913. 2. Slaves. 3. African Americans—Biography. 4. Women—Biography. 5. Underground railroad. 6. Antislavery movements.] I. Benge, Geoff, 1954- II. Title.
E444.T82 B427 2002
973.7'115—dc21 2002003060

Sixth printing 2025

Printed in the United States of America

HEROES OF HISTORY

Abraham Lincoln
Alan Shepard
Ben Carson
Benjamin Franklin
Benjamin Rush
Billy Graham
Captain John Smith
Christopher Columbus
Clara Barton
Davy Crockett
Daniel Boone
Douglas MacArthur
Dwight Eisenhower
Elizabeth Fry
Ernest Shackleton
Frederick Douglass
George Washington
George Washington Carver
Harriet Tubman
John Adams
Laura Ingalls Wilder
Louis Zamperini
Meriwether Lewis
Milton Hershey
Orville Wright
Ronald Reagan
Theodore Roosevelt
Thomas Edison
William Bradford
William Penn
William Wilberforce
Winston Churhill

To Shayna Blount

May this story inspire you
as much as it has inspired us.

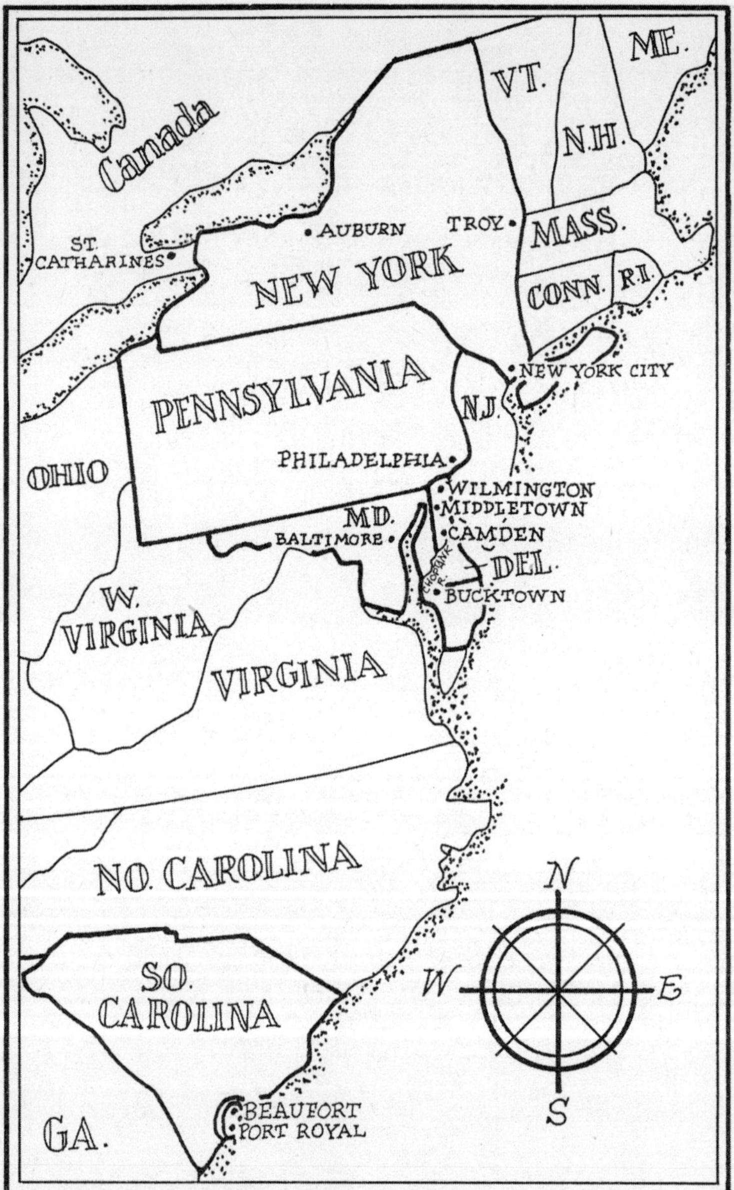

Canada
ME.
VT.
N.H.
MASS.
R.I.
CONN.
TROY
AUBURN
ST. CATHARINES
NEW YORK
NEW YORK CITY
PENNSYLVANIA
N.J.
PHILADELPHIA
OHIO
WILMINGTON
MIDDLETOWN
CAMDEN
MD.
BALTIMORE
DEL.
CHOPTANK R.
BUCKTOWN
W. VIRGINIA
VIRGINIA
NO. CAROLINA
SO. CAROLINA
BEAUFORT
PORT ROYAL
GA.
N
W
E
S

Contents

Chapter 1

"You Ain't Goin' Back"

"I can't go on, Moses!"

Harriet Tubman looked at the fear in Jim's eyes. She had seen it so many times before, heard the panic in his voice, sensed the tenseness of his limbs. And she understood his fear. She had felt it once, too, not knowing what lay ahead or how she would make it through while fretting over what might happen if she were caught. She understood it, but she had learned to overcome it. And that was what Jim was going to have to do. Now was not the time for doubts. They were only two days' travel from the plantation, still within range of the bloodhound that would be hot on their trail by now. They couldn't stop; Jim would just have to keep moving.

"Jim, we gotta keep movin'. Ain't no time to stop and worry. Come on. The good Lord, He's goin' with us. He'll see us through," Harriet said, trying to encourage her charge.

"No, Moses, I can't go on. I ain't never been this far from the plantation before. But somewhere somebody's gonna recognize me, I just know it. I can't go no farther. I gotta go back."

"Back, Jim? You know what they do to runaways," Harriet said.

"I knows. But if I go back and say, 'Master, I'm sorry. I don't know why I run off like that. Somethin' got the better of me. Ain't never gonna happen again. I'm ready to take a lickin' for what I done,' then maybe he's gonna go easy on me, beat me, and send me back out to the fields to work."

"Jim, you know that ain't gonna happen. Master—he's gonna make an example out of you. He's gonna whip you and brand you, and then he's gonna sell you south. Only thing you can do now is keep movin'," Harriet cajoled.

"I can't. My feet don't wanna move no more. How you know we gonna make it anyway? Plenty of runaways don't make it to freedom. Why you so sure we gonna make it?"

"I ain't lost nobody yet, and I don't intend to. Freedom's at the end of this road, Jim, and you gonna make it there. You ain't goin' back," Harriet said.

"Well, I ain't going on. I can't, I just can't."

"You got one choice, Jim, and that's movin' on. I ain't lettin' you go back. Too many people risked their lives to help you get this far, and I ain't about to let you go back and have some master beat out of you who they were. So we're gonna keep goin' through these woods and across the river so we can make it to the next station before dawn. I ain't beggin' no more, Jim. I'm tellin' you."

A surprised look spread across Jim's dark, moonlit face at the firmness of Harriet's last remark. "Moses, I can't."

"Then maybe this will help you, Jim." With that Harriet reached into her pocket and pulled out a silver pistol. She cocked the gun and aimed it at Jim. "Live north, Jim, or you're gonna die here."

Jim looked startled, as did the other three slaves Harriet was conducting north to freedom.

"I ain't scared to use it on you, Jim," Harriet said, looking down the muzzle at him, her hand steady as a rock.

"They said Moses is tough, and they's right," Jim muttered as Harriet stared at him.

Finally, after a long pause, Jim sighed, and without saying a word he turned and began walking north.

Harriet uncocked the pistol and slipped it back into her pocket. She knew that when they finally made it to freedom, Jim would thank her for not letting him go back. She had pulled the gun before on other runaways whose resolve had begun to waiver, and each time, after they had made it to freedom, they had thanked her for forcing them to go on.

As they walked on through the woods, Harriet thought back to when she had been a slave. Slavery was all about fear—fear of being whipped, fear of being sold south, fear of being separated from your family. Harriet hated using fear to push someone forward, but sometimes nothing else worked. She had been full of fear once herself as she escaped north alone. Now that she had tasted freedom, she wanted to take north as many other slaves as she could so that they could taste it, too. Sometimes doing that meant helping them overcome their fear.

Harriet had, in fact, made so many trips to the South to lead runaway slaves north to freedom that people began calling her Moses, an allusion to the biblical character who had led his people to freedom in the Promised Land. She did not mind the nickname, though leading people to freedom seemed very far removed from her life on the Brodas plantation in Dorchester County, Maryland. It had taken the first six years of her life to truly grasp the fate that awaited her. She still vividly recalled the day when it had all changed for her...

Chapter 2

"Big Changes a Comin' for You"

"When you gonna show me those puppies?" Harriet nagged her big brother Henry as he carried another load of wood past her and into the cookhouse.

Henry sighed. "If you want to see them, you'd better slip around the side door of the stable soon as I've finished up here. Reckon you can get away from Bella?"

Harriet grinned. "I ain't no baby!" she replied. "I can get out from under Bella's old eyes anytime I want to."

Henry shrugged. "If you say so. I can't wait around, though. The master's going out in his carriage this afternoon, and I have to harness the horses, so give me time to stack the wood and then come on around."

Harriet stood by the door to the cookhouse humming quietly between bites of corn bread. It was such a treat to be able to eat her own chunk of bread instead of the corn mush that Bella often served up in a long trough. When that happened, all of the children lined up around it and scooped the mush out with their hands in a desperate race to cram as much into their mouths as possible.

Several of the smaller children started to fuss. Bella, the toothless old black woman who looked after the children while their mothers worked, turned her attention to them. "Now hush," she scolded. "You make any more noise, and I'm gonna take you to the cotton fields and leave you there, and you ain't never gonna find your way home."

This pronouncement made one of the small boys cry. Seeing her opportunity to escape, Harriet kept her eyes on Bella as she inched her way toward the corner of the building. Finally she was out of sight. She turned and ran for the side door of the stables.

"Henry," she whispered, "you there?"

The door creaked open, and he beckoned her inside. It took Harriet a few moments to adjust to the darkness, and then she spotted them—a muddle of puppies climbing over one another in a box. She ran over to them and fell to her knees. She picked up one of the puppies and hugged it. "Oh, Henry, feel how soft its ears are. I wish I could have one."

"Well, that ain't gonna happen," Henry replied flatly. "They've been weaned off their mother, and they're all bein' sold tomorrow. A great bloodline, I heard the master say. Their mother's one of the best hounds in all of Dorchester County, maybe in all of Maryland. It's hard to imagine how such cute little critters can grow up to be a man's worst nightmare, ain't it?"

"What do you mean?" Harriet asked.

Henry rolled his big, brown eyes. "Sometimes you're slow as molasses in winter, Harriet. You walk around with your eyes on the sky, and you don't hardly notice what's going on around you. You ever hear the hounds yapping and howling in the night?"

"Well, yes," Harriet replied, "sometimes."

"Why you think that is?" Henry paused for a moment. "You don't think, and Old Rit's too scared to tell you, but they're after runaways."

"Runaways?" Harriet said.

"You know, slaves who try to steal away in the night or while the overseer is in the far-off field down by the river. Surely you know about the runaways?"

"I guess," Harriet said. She supposed she had heard the older folks talking about runaways, but they spoke in whispers, and her mother, Old Rit, usually shooed her away when they started talking in such low tones.

Harriet put the puppy down and picked up another one that had a black patch on his back and a white tail. "This is the one I'd like to keep," she said.

Henry shook his head. "You surely don't get it, do you? You and me and Old Rit and Ben, and all the black folks we know, we can't own anything. You got that?"

Harriet looked up at her brother, who had a faraway look in his eyes. Henry didn't seem to be talking to her anymore.

"You don't own the clothes you got on, and Old Rit don't own the blankets piled on the floor, or the cabin or the iron pot or the wooden spoons you eat with. None of us own anything, and we sure ain't ever gonna own a puppy." Henry paused for a moment and lowered his voice. "Someone's gotta tell you, girl. You're in for some big changes soon. Haven't you noticed you're the tallest one that Bella looks after? Soon there's gonna be some big changes a comin' for you."

Harriet put the puppy down. Suddenly all of the excitement of holding it had drained away, and she wanted to get back into the sunlight. She wiped her hands on her scratchy shirt and jumped up. "Gotta go," she said as she dashed for the door.

Harriet sneaked back to the other children, but now somehow she felt strangely alienated from them. Maybe Henry was right. She was a good half a head taller than the others. The afternoon continued on in the same manner as just about every other afternoon Harriet could recall. There were simple chores for her and some of the other girls to do: corn to shuck for dinner, wood to stack at the back of the cookhouse, and black-eyed peas to sort through. Halfway through the afternoon Harriet lugged a bucket of water to the cotton field for the workers there to drink. But her mind was not on the simple, everyday things. She could not get what Henry had told her out of her mind.

Big changes a comin'? What big changes? The question played over and over in her mind, and she thought about some of the other children who used to be with Bella. There was Belah, who went away to work for a doctor in Georgia, and Solomon, who was so sullen that Old Rit said he had been "sold down the river," whatever that meant. Somehow Harriet had never connected the fate of the older children in the quarters with her own. It seemed so silly now to imagine that she could go on staying with the little ones and Bella forever. Of course. She was going to be put to work soon. How could she have been so stupid as to not have seen it coming?

This new thought took root in Harriet as surely as the oak trees rooted themselves deep in the ground, and it would not let her go.

That night, as everyone squatted on the hard dirt floor of the cabin, Harriet listened, really listened to what the older folks were saying. "Johnny says there's three more wanted posters up for runaways from the plantation," someone said.

"How much reward they offerin'?" another asked.

"Up to six hundred dollars for La Verde. His master's real mad at him for runnin' off. If he gets caught, he'll have his ears sliced off for sure, and that won't be the worst of it."

"Sent out the hounds, they have," Harriet's father, Ben, said. "Better start prayin' he makes it."

A strong breeze sent a billow of smoke back down the chimney and into the room. As Harriet turned her face toward the wall, where fresh air seeped in between the logs, she thought about the puppies and how much she would love to own one. But Henry was right. What did she own? She had a special tree that was hers, or at least she told herself it was. It had long, low limbs and pretty cones. On the special occasions when she was allowed to take a message to her father, Harriet would stop at the tree and climb into its lowest branches. Just for a moment, she would feel completely engulfed in greenness. Then she would jump down and run to find her father. But Harriet had never told anyone the tree belonged to her, and she never would. It was her secret. Finally, thinking about her tree with its wide, welcoming branches and its fresh, clean smell, Harriet drifted off to sleep.

The following morning Harriet was up before dawn with everyone else. She watched as her older sister MaryAnn folded the blankets and set them against one wall. That gave everyone enough space to walk around inside. Harriet's mother stirred a pot of mush over the fire, and Harriet could hear her father sharpening the blade of his ax against a wetting stone. This morning there was time for breakfast. Often, though, the overseer blew his whistle early, and everyone would make a dash for the fields, leaving his or her breakfast behind.

Harriet walked as far as Bella's hut with her mother, who was headed for the big house.

"Been waitin' for you," Bella said through the open doorway. "Here, take Tom outside and gather the others. I'll be out soon. Make sure no one goes near the creek."

Tom ran across the floor and out the door, where he plunked himself down beside Harriet. She crouched down and picked up a stone. "Look what I can do!" she said in her most excited voice. She then placed the stone on the back of her hand, flipped it into the air, and caught it on the back of her other hand. "Bet you can't do that."

The toddler took the stone and promptly put it in his mouth.

"No, no," laughed Harriet. "That's not what you do."

She showed Tom her trick again. Just then, a shadow fell over her. She looked up and saw Jake, the houseboy, standing over her. Jake lived two cabins down from Harriet.

"Master says he wants you, and that you better look sharp," Jake said.

Harriet felt her heart pounding under her shirt. The master had never asked for her before. What could he want?

Bella poked her head out of the cabin. "What's up?" she asked Jake.

"Master wants Harriet. Some white lady's here in a carriage," he replied. "Don't know more than that."

Bella shook her head. "I done seen it comin', I did." Then she looked at Harriet. "Look lively, girl!" she said. "The master don't take well to being kept waiting. You'll get a whippin' if you linger."

Harriet threw the stone she was holding under the cabin and followed Jake to the big house. She clasped her hands behind her back so that no one would see them trembling.

Sure enough, the master, Edward Brodas, was standing on the porch with a white woman. "Make it quick!" he yelled.

Jake broke into a run, and Harriet followed. Soon they were standing on the bottom step.

"Come up here, girl," Edward said, beckoning to Harriet. "Jake, go water the mistress's horses."

"Yes, sir," Jake replied as he sprinted away, leaving Harriet to climb the steps alone.

"So, how old would you say she is?" Harriet heard the woman ask the master.

Edward stepped forward and put his hand on Harriet's chin. "Open up," he ordered.

Harriet opened her mouth. The master talked right over her head. "She's missing both front teeth, so she's five or six. I seem to recollect she was born around seedtime, but I couldn't be sure. Her mother, Old Rit, has a brood of them. Good stock," he said with a laugh.

Harriet felt her face grow hot. She wished more than anything that she could be in her tree.

"As I told you earlier, she's not house-trained," Edward went on, motioning for the woman to sit down. "But you get what you pay for, and she is going cheap."

"Yes," the woman replied dryly, "she's a scrawny thing." As she spoke, she squeezed Harriet's arm so tightly it took Harriet's breath away. "Let's hope she's a quick enough learner to meet my needs."

"I don't see why she shouldn't be. Her father's one of my best workers—strong, dependable, and one hundred percent honest. Word is that Ben's never told a lie, and I wouldn't doubt it. I'm sure she'll work out," Edward said.

The woman nodded. "Very well, then. Give me the papers to sign and I'll take her."

Twenty minutes later Harriet was seated on a wagon pulled by the two horses Jake had just watered. "You can call me Miss Cook," the woman said coldly. "I expect you to do whatever I tell you and never answer me back." She turned and grabbed Harriet by the shoulders. "You understand that, girl? Never answer me back."

Harriet nodded and looked away. In the distance she could see the women from the quarters bent over the young cotton crop. "Weedin' time," she had heard one of them complain that morning. She could see Jake's mother, with her blue striped bandana, and Aunt Milly but not her mother. Old Rit did not work in the fields. Instead, she did the washing in the big house, a never-ending round of tablecloths, napkins, sheets, and petticoats. Harriet wondered whether she would ever see her mother again. Where was this white woman with the cold voice and vicelike grasp taking her?

Everything inside Harriet wanted to jump from the wagon and run to the women in the field, but she dared not do something so rash. Instead, silent hot tears coursed down her cheeks as her brother's words came tumbling back to her. *You're in for some big changes. You don't own nothin', not the clothes on your back, not even the wooden spoon you eat with."*

The wagon rumbled on down the road, past the edge of the cotton fields, over the bridge, and into the woods where Harriet's father supervised a gang of slaves cutting down trees. The logs would then be sent down the river to Chesapeake Bay, where they would be loaded onto boats destined for Baltimore, where they would be used to build ships. Harriet knew this because once, about two harvests before, she had been allowed to go with her father when he took the logs downriver. She loved every minute of that trip, from the salty smell of the marshes to sitting on her father's broad shoulders as the boat captain handed him a bill of sale for the logs. That was the only time Harriet had been off the Brodas property—until now.

Suddenly the rhythmic chant of a work gang brought Harriet back to the present. As the wagon rounded a corner in the road, she spotted her father and his crew. The men were chopping the limbs from an enormous tree they had just felled. Her father stood poised to swing the ax when he turned around. Harriet caught her breath as he looked right at her. She saw a frozen look of terror in his eyes, and then he shook his head and looked away. Harriet twisted around in her seat, eager to fix one last image of Ben in her mind. He was kneeling on the ground, his head down and his shoulders slumped. Harriet guessed he was praying for her. It was something he did a lot of.

The rest of the trip was a blur. Under other circumstances Harriet would have been looking every which way, trying to take it all in, but now she hardly noticed the landscape passing before her eyes. All she could think of was that each roll of the wagon's wheels was taking her farther from the only home she had ever known and the only people who had ever loved her. Whatever lay ahead now was unimaginable.

Chapter 3

One of the Lucky Ones

"How many times do I have to show you, you stupid little girl?" Mrs. Cook spat as she lunged at Harriet. "You can't wind the yarn tightly like that! If I have to stop to untangle one more spool, you won't get anything to eat tonight. You hear me?"

Harriet nodded. Her eyes lowered and her shoulders slumped slightly forward. It had taken only a couple of days for her to figure out that this was the best thing to do when she was yelled at or struck across the face. Any other kind of reaction only seemed to invite more anger.

By now Harriet cared little whether or not she got anything to eat that night. Her stomach was so churned up from missing her family that food did not sit well in it. She wished she had some of Old

Rit's herb potion. It always seemed to settle her stomach, or at least it had in the past. Now Harriet wondered whether anything could clear the knot in her stomach and make her feel like her old self.

The Cooks' house was not like the big house at all. It was more like one of the cabins in the slaves' quarters, except that it had two windows, a woodstove, and a huge linen loom that took up nearly half the floor space. The loom, which Harriet had first imagined to be something interesting, had turned out to be a nightmare. Mrs. Cook sat at the loom for hours each day, throwing the shuttle back and forth and cursing when the thread snapped or tangled. Harriet's job was to keep Mrs. Cook supplied with bobbins wound with thread, not too loose and not too tight.

The task proved to be impossible. By the end of Harriet's first day her hands were covered with cuts from the harsh flax fiber. As the bobbin filled up, the thread got tighter, and as much as Harriet tried not to let it happen, it always did. It was then that the beatings began, until Harriet's hands shook so much, she could hardly hold the thread, much less wind it to her mistress's exact requirements.

Nighttime became Harriet's only friend. At least then, as she lay on a pile of rags on the kitchen floor, Harriet could be alone with her thoughts. She liked to think about the wonderful stories Old Rit told during the long winter evenings. The story of Moses was her favorite. "That old Moses," Old Rit would say, "he didn't never give up. Even though Pharaoh says the children of Israel can't go free, old Moses, he says 'Let my people go, or see how the Lord's gonna move you on out of the way. He gonna move you out of the way, I tell you, he gonna move you out of the way!'"

There were other stories, too, about God parting the sea so that Moses could lead his people across, and one about little bits of fine, white, fluffy bread falling from the sky when the people got hungry.

These stories were fine to recall in the night, but when the sun came up and Harriet ran outside to draw water from the well, the cycle of winding bobbins and being beaten would soon begin again. With every breath Harriet took, she prayed that things would change, and a week after she started with Mrs. Cook they did.

"I can't stand her one more moment!" Mrs. Cook burst out when her husband walked through the door. "She costs me more time and money than she saves. And she makes my blood boil so that I can hardly do my weaving. If ever God created a useless Negro, it was this one."

Harriet put her head down and continued to wind the thread the best way she knew how.

"Well, if she's useless inside, I'll try her outdoors. After lunch I have to check the muskrat traps. If she could be trained to do that, I suppose it would be something."

"Oh, take her. I don't care if she drowns in one of the traps!" Mrs. Cook snapped back.

Soon Harriet found herself standing on the bank of a large stream.

Mr. Cook pointed at the water. "See, there's a line down there with a wooden float on it," he said. "Your job is to get into the water and follow the line. Under each float is a muskrat trap. You got to feel around and see if there's an animal in the trap. If there is, you pull it out like this and stick it in the sack, see?"

Harriet watched and nodded silently as Mr. Cook took a metal clamp out of a knapsack and showed her how to release it. Her mind was full of questions she dare not ask: Would the muskrats be alive? Would they bite or claw her? How deep was the water, and how long was the line?

In the next few weeks, Harriet learned the answers to all these questions. She learned that the muskrat trap kept the muskrat underwater so that it drowned long before she retrieved it. The water she had to wade in sometimes came up as high as her neck, and Harriet dreaded touching the beautiful, dead creatures. Despite this Harriet was glad to be outside. Sometimes as she wandered along the bank of the stream on her way home, she found herself humming. There was something about the feeling of the sun on her back, the blades of grass between her toes, and the chirping of the crickets that made her feel free. The squirrels that scampered up the trees did not know she was a slave girl, nor did the ducks and the snipes that flew overhead.

As the weeks went on, Harriet decided that she would never work inside a house again. She promised herself that somehow she would find a way to be outside in nature. However, this proved to be a difficult promise to keep. One morning Harriet woke up with a splitting headache. She stumbled out to the well, but the morning sunlight stung her eyes and sent her reeling. As she spun, she felt the slap of a hand against her cheek.

"Hurry up, you useless girl," Mrs. Cook chided. "It shouldn't take you half an hour to draw water. I am waiting for my coffee."

Harriet stumbled through her morning tasks, too afraid to tell Mrs. Cook how awful she felt but equally afraid she would collapse. Later that morning Mr. Cook half dragged her to the far end of the property and ordered her to check the muskrat traps.

"Ain't no use pretending to be sick," he said. "I wasn't born yesterday. I know every Negro trick that was ever invented. You're no sicker than I am."

Harriet took a deep breath and stepped into the water. The muddy bottom squelched between her toes. She looked down. The water turned into a brown swirling blur, and then she fell forward.

Sift the meal and gimme the husk.
Bake the cake and gimme the crust.
Fry the pork and gimme the skin.
Ask me when I'm coming again.
Juber, Juber Juber-ee.

Harriet lay flat on her back, trying to think. Was that her mother's voice singing to her, and was that the smell of hotcakes being baked over the cabin fire? She tried to lift her head, but it would not budge.

"I think she's waking up!" It was her sister MaryAnn's voice.

"God almighty be praised!" Harriet heard Old Rit reply.

Relief flooded Harriet's mind. She was home again.

It was several days before she was well enough to sit up and hear the whole story. After she had fainted into the water, Mr. Cook had pulled her out and taken her back to the house, where she lay unconscious. Mrs. Cook was too disgusted with Harriet to try to help her in any way, but news got back to the Brodas farm that Harriet was ill, and Mr. Brodas had sent Ben to fetch her. "Worth more to me alive than dead," he had said.

"But I thought I belonged to the Cooks," Harriet said. "Did Master Brodas buy me back?"

Old Rit reached out and held her hand. "No, child. You was one of the lucky ones. You wasn't sold. You was hired out to the Cooks. They paid the master for your labor by the week, though I hear Mrs. Cook did nothing but complain you weren't worth what she and her husband had to pay." Old Rit lowered her voice. "Harriet, now that you're worth money, you got to walk a fine line. If you're too stubborn to work for hire, you'll be sold south like the others and we'll never see you again."

Harriet nodded. At six years old, she was beginning to understand the precarious position she was in.

No sooner had Harriet arrived back in the slave cabin than she broke out in spots. Her body was covered from head to toe. She had the measles and a bad case of bronchitis from hours of wading in the cold, waist-deep water. As Harriet recovered, her mother tended to her needs, plying her with herbal potions and massaging her chest. All the while Harriet tried not to think about what might happen once she was better. Slowly, bit by bit, with Old Rit's constant attention, Harriet began to regain her strength.

One day MaryAnn came back from the big house with news from the outside. "Mr. Mowberry came by and said that Thomas Jefferson died last week."

"Must have been an old man by now," Ben commented.

"Yep," MaryAnn continued. "Said he was eighty-three years old, and he died on the Fourth of July."

"Fourth of July, 1826," mumbled Old Rit. "And we still ain't no closer to bein' free. If I could just get someone to listen to me, we'd all be free. All of us!"

Harriet looked away. She hated to hear the particular combination of despair and bitterness that crept into her mother's voice when she talked of freedom. According to Old Rit, her last master had promised to free her—or manumit her, as it was called—when he died. Old Rit always maintained that he had told her it was all legal and written into his will. But when the old man died, Old Rit was sold, and nothing more was ever said about freedom. "No chance to uncover the truth," she would say sometimes. "How does an old Negro like me challenge a rich white family? Why, I couldn't even read the will if it were placed in front of me, but I know what I heard, and I know I should be free."

Harriet had heard the story many times, and she believed it. If your mother was a slave, then you were a slave, and if your mother was a free black, then you were free, too. So if the will were ever followed, Harriet would be free along with all of her brothers and sisters.

"Ain't never gonna happen in our lifetime," Henry grumbled. "Our chance at freedom's come and gone."

As Harriet lay recovering, she thought a lot about owning people and freedom and all that it meant. How wonderful it would be to keep the family together without worrying about someone being sold down the river or hired out to catch his or her death of cold.

Even though no one talked about it, Harriet knew that when she recovered, she would be hired out again. She prayed that she would get a kind master who would let her do outside chores and give her shoes to wear in winter. None of these came to pass.

The hiring process happened much as it had the previous time. Harriet was summoned to the big house and introduced to Miss Susan, another white stranger. Soon she was sitting on a wagon bound for an unknown destination. Two hours later they pulled up in front of a medium-sized house. A woman sat on the veranda holding a baby.

"That's Rupert," Miss Susan said. "Your job is to look after him. If he cries, I will hold you responsible. I hate to listen to a crying baby, especially at night. There is nothing worse than having a good night's sleep disrupted by too much noise." She climbed down from the wagon and turned to Harriet. "Well, come on, girl. I didn't hire you to have you sit idly about."

The woman with the baby came to greet them. "She's a bit small, isn't she, Susan?" she asked as she examined Harriet. "Couldn't you get someone a little bigger?"

"She'll do fine," Miss Susan snapped. "You'll see. The secret is to get them young and train them to your liking." She reached down and pulled Harriet's ear. "You'll do everything I say, won't you, girl?"

"Yes, missus," Harriet replied as the familiar lump solidified in her stomach.

Harriet spent the rest of the day with Rupert, a large, fat baby about as different from the shape of a slave baby as Harriet could imagine. Rupert smiled and cooed but did not talk yet, and he could sit up but not crawl. Most of the time he sat in Harriet's lap as she sang him songs and played with his pudgy little fingers.

When night came, Harriet discovered the true terror of watching a white baby. Miss Susan tucked Rupert into his cradle and pointed to a shelf just above it. "There's a whip on that shelf," she said to Harriet, "and if I have to come into this room to tend to the baby, you'll be feeling its full force. Have I made myself clear?"

Harriet nodded. "Yes, missus," she muttered, looking down at Rupert.

It was the longest night of Harriet's life. She sat beside the cradle, rocking it gently. She dared not fall asleep in case Rupert woke up. Every so often she stood up and stretched or pinched herself to keep from falling asleep. By the following morning, when Miss Susan came into the nursery, Harriet was so tired she felt sick.

"I will feed Rupert in the mornings," Miss Susan announced in a cheerful voice. "You can help my sister, Miss Emily, with the housework." She raised her eyebrows. "And mind, I am particular about the house, so no skimping on the polishing or not sweeping in the corners." She picked Rupert up. "Well, go on, girl. Don't dawdle. You can start by sweeping and dusting the dining room."

Harriet stood up and raced downstairs to the dining room. It was the grandest room she had ever been inside, with its two glass windows, six matching chairs around a table, and a rug on the floor.

"Sweep and dust," she said to herself, frantically trying to think how she should go about it. She had helped her mother sweep out the cabin before, but what was dusting? Unsure of the answer, Harriet decided to look for a broom and begin with sweeping.

She found a broom in the kitchen, propped up against a table with a bowl of peaches on it. The sight of the peaches reminded Harriet that she had not eaten since the night before, but she knew better than to take anything from the kitchen. She would get fed when the mistress felt like feeding her. Trying to ignore her rumbling stomach, Harriet carried the broom into the dining room and began sweeping the rug.

A minute later Miss Susan entered the room. "You stupid girl!" she screamed. "What do you think you are doing, sweeping the rug! Don't you know you should take it outside and beat it. You are stirring up the dust in here, and I will not have dust everywhere. If I come back and find so much as a speck of dust in here, I'll give you a whipping you'll never forget," she said as she stormed out of the room.

Harriet stood there, her hands trembling, tears forming in the corners of her eyes. All she wanted to do was curl up in the corner and sleep, but she dragged the chairs off the rug so that she could take it outside and beat it.

Miss Susan came back twenty minutes later, her face white with fury. "You must be the stupidest creature God ever made," she fumed as she ran her finger over the top of the china cabinet. "Look at this. Pure filth." Then she pulled a whip out of her skirt pocket and lashed at Harriet.

Harriet screamed in terror as the whip cut into the back of her neck. She raised her hands to protect her head, but Miss Susan yanked them down to her sides and kept lashing her. Soon there was a puddle of blood on the floor, but even then Miss

Susan continued with the whipping. Harriet began to wonder if she had gone mad.

Finally Harriet heard another voice. "Stop it, Susan. Stop it at once. Can't you see the girl's been hurt enough."

The whirl of the whip stopped, and for a moment everything was silent. Harriet turned to see Miss Emily standing in the doorway.

"For goodness' sake," Miss Emily said to her sister, "think about what you are doing. If you maim the girl, you'll never get any work out of her and you'll lose your deposit when you return her to Mr. Brodas. What was the problem, anyway?"

"She won't even sweep or dust properly," Miss Susan replied, glaring at Harriet.

Miss Emily took a deep breath. "She may never have been taught how. Let me show her how to do a few things around the house. I'm sure she is capable of following directions if they are specific enough. After all, she must be at least six years old."

"Very well," Miss Susan replied grudgingly, "but mind you, don't spoil her. I won't have an uppity Negro in the house."

"Come on, Harriet," Miss Emily said. "Go out to the creek and wash yourself. You're dripping blood on the floor."

Ten minutes later Harriet was sitting beside the stream, an old, wet towel wadded up around her neck.

"You must do your best," Miss Emily told her. "My sister has an unfortunate temper, and she is used to having her way."

"If you'll show me what to do, I'll try as hard as I can," Harriet said.

The day seemed to grow longer and longer, and it was not until the sun went down that Harriet was given a drink of milk and a chunk of corn bread to eat. She was almost too tired to eat it, especially as she contemplated the long night rocking the baby's cradle that was yet to come.

Night and day followed each other in a blur of crying baby, whippings, and sweeping. Harriet's neck became crisscrossed with scars, new ones forming on top of old ones that had not completely healed.

Hardly a day went by that Miss Susan did not explode in anger, especially once Miss Emily went away and it was just Miss Susan, her husband, Mr. Jake, and the baby living in the house.

One morning, when Harriet had been in the house about two months, things became unbearable.

"Get in here," Harriet heard Miss Susan call her.

Harriet propped the broom up against the wall and hurried into the kitchen, where Miss Susan and Mr. Jake were in the middle of a particularly nasty argument.

"If I've told you once, I've told you a thousand times, you're a fool to trust that neighbor of ours," Miss Susan yelled. "If you had listened to me, we wouldn't be in this financial mess, you fool!"

Harriet stood silently between the door and the kitchen table. It seemed that Miss Susan had forgotten about her completely. As Miss Susan continued to scream at her husband, Harriet's eyes were drawn to the sugar bowl on the table. In it was a neat arrangement of sugar cubes. Miss Susan stood with her back to Harriet and was wildly flailing her arms.

Suddenly Harriet had a bold thought. What if she slipped her hand out and took a sugar cube? She could almost taste it melting in her mouth. She edged closer to the table, never taking her eyes off her mistress. Then she reached out her hand and picked up a sugar cube.

At that exact moment Miss Susan swung around and took in the entire situation. Every ounce of her anger transferred from Mr. Jake to Harriet. "Why, you little thief!" she yelled. "I'll whip you to within an inch of your life, so help me God."

Harriet watched transfixed as Miss Susan reached for the rawhide whip that she kept on a shelf above the woodstove.

Without even thinking, Harriet turned and ran out the door. Her legs pumped automatically as she sprinted down the driveway and out of sight, far too frightened to give any thought to what she had done or what would happen to her now.

Chapter 4

Not Worth Sixpence

Harriet ran and ran until her legs began to feel wobbly under her. It was then that she noticed the pigpen. She stumbled over to it. Inside she saw a large sow and ten piglets. But what caught Harriet's eyes were the potato peelings in the trough at the back of the pen. Seeing them made her suddenly aware of the gnawing hunger in her stomach. Before she knew it, she had scaled the fence around the pen and was scooping potato peels from the trough into her mouth. The sow grunted and tried to push Harriet away with her nose. Harriet grabbed one last handful of potato peels and retreated to the far corner of the pen.

From Friday until the following Tuesday, Harriet sat in the corner of the pen, ignoring the wretched smell and grabbing a few handfuls of potato peels when she thought the sow was not looking. Hopelessness flooded over her. All the stories of runaway slaves she had heard in the family cabin at night came flooding back to Harriet. She thought about the slaves who had been captured and had their ears cut off and the men who were branded with a big *R* on their chests to mark them as runaways and in need of close attention and harsh treatment from their overseers. Would the same fate await her now that she had fled?

By Tuesday Harriet knew she had to do something. She was terrified the sow would trample her while she slept, and she was constantly hungry. She realized that she would eventually have to return to Miss Susan's and face the consequences of her actions. Later that day she climbed out of the pigpen and walked back to the house. Harriet knew she stunk terribly, and her long skirt was ripped to shreds.

Miss Susan was furious when Harriet arrived at the door. Her voice quivered as she called for her husband. "Harriet's back, the ungrateful little wretch. Come and whip her for me. I don't trust myself not to kill her after the humiliation she's caused me."

When the beating was over, Harriet was dumped into the back of the wagon, and Miss Susan drove off with her.

Harriet lay on the floor of the wagon, bloodied, bruised, and still covered with mud. She desperately wanted a drink of water, but she was too afraid to ask for one. Finally the tall, broad oak trees of the Brodas farm came into view. Relief flooded through Harriet. She knew she would soon be seeing Old Rit and Ben.

"Get down," Miss Susan growled. "Come on. Stop making such a performance. You can walk."

Slowly Harriet got to her feet and found her balance. "You can have the little devil," she heard Miss Susan say to Mr. Brodas. "As far as I'm concerned, she's not worth sixpence."

Mr. Brodas glared at Harriet. "Nothing but trouble, that one," he agreed.

Harriet was beyond caring whether she was in trouble or not. Her head throbbed, and she longed to be lying down in her own cabin. Soon she got her wish, and Old Rit hovered over her, washing her clean and applying boiled leaves to the wounds the whip had inflicted on her body.

Every so often Harriet let out a whimper, and she tried to keep her eyes open so that she could fix her mother's image in her mind. Once when Harriet's eyes were closed, she overheard her parents talking in low voices.

"That girl's got pluck," she heard her father say.

"Enough pluck to get her killed most likely," her mother replied. "Ain't no point in a slave girl having pluck. It'd be better if she learned to smile and say 'yes, missus, no, missus' like MaryAnn does. Lord knows pluck is a dangerous thing."

"What do you reckon's gonna happen to her?" Old Rit asked. "The master surely can't keep hiring her out. I'd say she won't get another chance in a big house."

"Probably right. Let's pray she stays around here," Ben said.

There was a long silence. Harriet knew that her parents were both thinking of Bessy and Moss, her two older sisters who had been marched south on a chain gang when they were about Harriet's age.

Harriet spent many hours thinking about this possibility, but thankfully it did not come to pass. This time, once she was strong enough, Harriet was hired out to a nearby plantation as a general farmhand. She learned how to hitch a plow and run a straight furrow, how to weed tobacco and pick cotton. From the time she was eight years old, Harriet was expected to do a man's work, and she was whipped when she fell short. Even so, she was grateful to be outside in the open. She loved to watch the leaves changing color in the fall and the wild geese fly north in their perfect *V* formations.

Sometimes at night Harriet would stand outside the cabin she shared with several other women. "You lookin' at that North Star again?" they would ask. "Sure am," Harriet would reply, gazing up at the one star that seemed to stand in the same place while every other star drifted through the night sky. "One day I'm gonna follow that star." "Ha," the others would laugh, "where's a slip of a girl like you gonna get the courage to do a foolish thing like that?"

Harriet did not answer their teasing. She simply smiled and promised herself that one day she would make it to the almost mythical North, where all black people were free and people were paid for their labor. Maybe she would even ride the new Underground Railroad black folks were talking about.

Harriet didn't quite know what to make of this Underground Railroad. She had heard the story of Tice Davids, a young slave from Kentucky who had escaped from his master and planned to cross the Ohio River at the town of Ripley. However, his master pursued him with dogs and was soon about to catch up with him. So Tice Davids had jumped into the river and headed for the far shore. His master rounded up a boat and followed, but in those few minutes, Tice disappeared, never to be heard from again. Since he was a good swimmer, it seemed unlikely that he had drowned. Lacking any explanation for how a slave could have disappeared right under his nose, the master told everyone that Tice Davids must have taken an Underground Railroad.

Was it true? Did a train rumble along somewhere under Harriet's feet, taking anyone who dared to seek freedom? Harriet didn't know, but it was something she was determined to find out one day.

During the cotton harvest of 1831, Harriet heard an even more astounding story. This story involved a slave who did not try to escape north. Instead, he did something unthinkable—he led a slave revolt against white plantation owners. The man, whose name was Nat Turner, lived in Southampton, Virginia. News that he and six followers had killed sixty white men, women, and children and liberated hundreds of slaves spread like wildfire across the South. Slave owners turned white with fear at the thought that their own slaves might rise up and kill them, while slaves were inspired by the courage and success of a few of their own.

For days little else was talked about. Local militia and federal troops flooded the area, determined to put down the uprising. With their superior weapons and numbers, this did not take long, and in the process over a hundred slaves were killed. But when everything had died down, Nat Turner was still at large. Every slave working in the field kept watch for him, and rumors soon began to circulate that he, too, had taken the Underground Railroad to freedom.

Eventually, though, this rumor proved to be false, and Nat Turner was captured in a dirt cave not far from his old plantation. He was tried and sentenced to be hanged.

Once the hanging was over, however, things did not return to normal. Harriet knew it, and so did the other slaves. Something had changed. Plantation owners, including Mr. Brodas and the man Harriet was hired out to, were very nervous. Other countries, like Mexico, had outlawed slavery, and the slaves in Haiti had recently overthrown their French masters and declared themselves a black republic.

The fear white slave owners now had meant changes for the slaves. It was no longer acceptable for two or three slaves to be seen talking to one another, and slaves were forced to sing while they worked in the fields. Slave owners took comfort in the thought that a singing slave was not a talking slave, since talking could lead to the planning of another uprising. Also, black people could no longer hold church services without a white person present to listen for signs of trouble. Sunday schools were banned in case slave children became inspired by stories of Moses and Daniel, and it became a crime punishable by death to teach a slave to read or write. Guards were placed on all forms of public transport, and papers were required to cross every bridge in the South. At all cost, slaves were to be kept ignorant and uninformed about the world around them.

Despite the new, harsher laws governing slaves, all of the activity surrounding Nat Turner fired Harriet with a sense of hope. Surely the times were changing. One group of people could not hold another group of people in bondage forever.

Sometimes Cudjoe, an old black man who was in charge of the master's wardrobe, would smuggle a newspaper out of the big house. Cudjoe had learned to read as a young boy, and the slaves gathered in his cabin to hear the latest news about their collective fate.

One night, soon after Nat Turner had been executed, Harriet sat by the fire at Cudjoe's side.

"Ain't no way we can let them win," the old man said. "Just ain't no way. We knows too much now." With these words he pulled a newspaper from under his shirt. "Listen to this—it's from a speech in the legislature in Virginia." He cleared his throat and tilted the newspaper toward the open fire for light. "'We have as far as possible closed every avenue by which light may enter slaves' minds. If we could extinguish the capacity to see the light, our work would be completed; they would then be on a level with the beasts of the field.' Ha!" spat Cudjoe. "That ain't never gonna happen. We have the same light from God as any man of any other color, and some of them knows it. Listen to this bit."

Cudjoe turned the page of the newspaper. "This is about the opinion of a white man named Henry Berry. He says, 'Pass as severe laws as you will to keep those unfortunate creatures in ignorance; it is in vain unless you can extinguish that spark of intellect which God has given them....Can man be in the midst of freedom and not know what freedom is? A death struggle must come in which one or the other class is extinguished forever.' See," Cudjoe went on, "there's plenty of white men out there who can see the writing on the wall as clear as Belshazzar in the Bible. They just don't want to give up their property, that's all. Pure greed. We's in chains because of men's greed. But it ain't gonna last forever. No sirree, it sure ain't. God is gonna set us free."

The more Harriet heard words like these, the more convinced she became that one day she would be free. She took to praying and singing at the same time, using the old songs her parents had taught her to express her hope. One of her favorites went like this:

Didn't my Lord deliver Daniel,
Deliver Daniel, deliver Daniel?
Didn't my Lord deliver Daniel,
And why not every man?
He delivered Daniel from the lions' den,
Jonah from the belly of the whale,
And the Hebrew children from the fiery furnace,
Why not every man?

And why not every man? The line from the song echoed in Harriet's mind as she split logs for the fire and urged on the oxen pulling the plow.

"I'm gonna make a run for it during the corn husking tonight," one of Harriet's fellow slaves told her one day as they worked side by side picking corn.

"You sure, Jim?" Harriet said, her eyes darting back and forth to make sure the overseer hadn't noticed them talking. "You've been caught twice already. I reckon if you fail again, the master's bound to sell you south."

"I reckon so, too, so I better not fail!" Jim said with a wink. "I'm gonna find me that Underground Railroad they all talk about."

"Really?" Harriet replied. "You think you can?"

"I'm gonna try. I hear there are white people all along the road north who gladly give help to run-away slaves. You just have to ask the right ones—that's the trick to it."

"Sounds risky to me," Harriet said, half wishing she had the courage to ask to join him.

"You just wait and see. Tonight when the shuckin' party's under way, I'll be off."

Harriet felt a lump in her stomach for the remainder of the day. She did not know why. After all, Jim was in charge of his own fate, and it had little to do with her. Still, she had worked beside Jim for several years and had grown attached to her quick-thinking friend.

That night there was a huge shucking party. Slaves from several nearby plantations came to help with the work, just as Harriet and the other slaves would cross over to the neighbors and help them shuck corn in the nights to follow. It was a time Harriet normally looked forward to. The slaves would hold shucking races among themselves, and when the work was done, the powerful singers would take turns mounting the huge pile of cornhusks and entertain everyone with funny songs. However, this night, as the moon rose high in the sky, Harriet felt so nervous she did not join in the normal banter. Instead, she kept her eye on Jim.

When the shucking pile was about half done, Harriet watched Jim slip quietly to the back of the group and then break into a sprint across the corn-stubbled fields. Her hands trembled as she watched the overseer. Suddenly he gave a shout. "Hey, where's Jim?"

Everyone stopped working and waited to see what would happen next. The overseer jerked his head toward the field. Harriet followed his gaze in horror. Her friend's white shirt was still visible in the moonlit field.

"Why, the black devil!" the overseer yelled, reaching for his whip. "I'll teach him a lesson he'll never forget." He leapt up and raced after Jim.

Without thinking about what she was doing, Harriet threw the pile of corn off her knees and sprinted after him. Years of working outside had made her fit and fast, and she easily kept up with the overseer.

Harriet was out of breath when they reached a small store at the crossroads. As she neared it, she caught sight of Jim inside talking to another black man. The overseer saw him too and raced in and blocked the door. "Got you!" he yelled as Harriet raced up behind him. He turned and saw her. "Quick," he said, "hold Jim down, and I'll whip him to within an inch of his life right here."

Harriet looked up and with a steady gaze met the wild look in Jim's eyes. "Yes, master," she replied, stepping closer to the overseer, who had walked inside and cornered Jim.

With all the calmness she possessed, Harriet ran over to Jim and grabbed him by the arms. Even though she was only thirteen years old, she was strong enough to hold him.

"Good girl," encouraged the overseer. "Bring him over here."

Harriet pulled Jim roughly toward the door and then loosened her grip on him. "Go now!" she whispered urgently. "I'll stop him."

After a second's hesitation, she felt Jim pull away from her as he ran out the door.

"Why the..." Harriet heard the overseer yell as he raced to follow Jim. Harriet beat him to the door and stood in front of it, her arms outstretched to prevent him from passing.

With a shocked look on his face, the overseer reached for the nearest thing he could find to throw at the escaping slave. He yelled an oath as he drew back his hand and hurled a two-pound weight from the store scales in the direction of Jim. The weight missed its mark. Harriet felt a thud on the left side of her head and heard her skull crack. Suddenly she saw a brilliant white light, and then everything went black and silent.

Chapter 5

He Would Never Ever Own Her Soul

It was nearly a week before Harriet opened her eyes again. She could see people moving around her—Old Rit cooing over her, her brother Henry gingerly daubing her head with a foul-smelling lotion—but she could not respond. She just lay there on a pile of rags in the corner of the cabin.

Slowly, over the next few days, Harriet began to lift her arms a little and nod at her family. Her head pounded incessantly, and she finally found the courage to raise her fingers to the side of her skull and feel the wound. As she ran her fingers over her left temple, Harriet felt a huge hole the size of a blackbird's egg. Her hand jerked back down to her side, and she shut her eyes to try to block out the horror of what she had just discovered. The two-pound weight had rammed right through her skull, and it was two days before Harriet dared to feel the gaping wound again.

In the meantime Harriet lay slipping in and out of consciousness. Sometimes she heard voices above her talking. "This is quite a girl you got here, Old Rit," she heard someone say. "Word of her has gone over the county line."

"That so?" her mother replied. "I guess I can believe that. Not every day a slave girl helps a man escape. Just hope he makes it to freedom and that he knows the sacrifice she made for him."

"Haven't heard nothin' of Jim, so he might have boarded that Underground Railroad and gone to freedom."

Harriet was relieved to hear this. All of the pain and suffering was worth it just to hear that she had helped her friend escape slavery.

Sometimes, as she lay in the corner of the cabin, Harriet had strange dreams. She dreamed of white ladies all dressed in filmy gowns standing beside a river in a field of beautiful flowers. The women beckoned her to come over the river. In her dreams Harriet always ran as fast as she could toward these women, but time after time she stumbled and fell on the riverbank. No matter how hard she tried, she could not get up and keep going. When she awoke from such dreams, Harriet was always sweating and her heart was pounding fast. She began to imagine that one day she would take that long journey into the outstretched, welcoming arms on the other side of the river.

"She ain't goin' nowhere for a long time," she heard Ben say one day. "I don't care. Master Brodas can bring a hundred buyers a day by here, but ain't none of them gonna buy Harriet. She's more dead than alive, and even a young 'un could see that."

"Well, he's bringin' 'em anyhow," Old Rit replied. "But you're right. None of them is nibbling on the bait."

Harriet lay thinking about what they were saying. It could mean only one thing. Even in such a terrible state, with her skull staved in and her inability to stand up, her master was trying to sell her! She groaned at the thought, and Old Rit rushed over to massage her neck and arms.

"They ain't gonna take me nowhere!" Harriet muttered. "I might be a slave on the outside, but I defied my overseer. I ain't gonna bend to them anymore!"

The thought sent a fire through Harriet's bones. Right there and then, she decided she was done with slavery. Mr. Brodas might be able to get her body to dig and plow and chop wood, but he would never ever own her soul. She would never smile or bow and scrape again. They could punish her any way they wanted—nothing could be worse than what she had just been through.

By Christmastime Harriet was able to sit up most of the day and even take a few steps outside the cabin, provided she leaned on the wall for support. Mr. Brodas kept bringing prospective buyers to see her, but by now Harriet had learned to roll her eyes back in her head and look half stupid when men came to look at her. Sadly, though, it was not all an act. As Harriet recovered from the terrible blow to her head, there were times when she fell into a deep, comalike sleep. This happened without warning, and it could last a minute or an hour. She had no way of telling how long she had been asleep. Sometimes she would fall asleep in the middle of a sentence or while leaning against a broom she was using to sweep out the cabin. Often when she awoke, people would be gathered around her staring. "There goes Harriet off again. Ain't never recovered from that crack on the head," someone would say.

Harriet knew they were probably right, but there was nothing she could do about it. The big indentation in her skull was another reminder of the price she had paid for Jim's freedom. Still she prayed that God would help her to accept her new problems. She also prayed that God would make Mr. Brodas a kind master and that he would stop hiring his slaves out to cruel men. When this prayer did not seem to work, Harriet took a new tack. She spent many long hours in the night asking God to kill Mr. Brodas if he would not change his ways.

Soon after Harriet started to pray for her master's death, Mr. Brodas became unexpectedly ill and died. Now Harriet was mortified. She had asked God to kill Mr. Brodas, and now he was dead. Although her common sense told her she had not caused Mr. Brodas's death, she still felt guilty about the prayers she had prayed.

As word of Mr. Brodas's death spread through the slave quarters, an air of panic set in. What would happen to them now? Who would their new master be? Would he decide it was time to change the way things were run on the plantation and sell some of them south? Would he keep the families together, or would he separate husbands, wives, and children to break down old patterns of loyalty? No one knew the answers to these questions, but everyone agreed that the death of a master could prove to be the most terrible event in a slave's life.

Thankfully things did not go too badly for Harriet's family. Mr. Brodas's son was too young to take over the farm, and so Dr. Anthony Thompson, a preacher from Bucktown, was appointed as his ward.

Dr. Thompson was not a cruel man, though he was interested in making as much money as he could from the slaves. He hired Harriet's father to a nearby builder named John Stewart, and in time Ben convinced Mr. Stewart to hire Harriet as well.

At first Harriet was very weak, able only to do simple chores around the house. In time her strength returned, and she asked to be allowed to join her father felling trees and dressing timber and working in Mr. Stewart's fields.

Mr. Stewart gave his permission, and he even allowed Harriet to hire herself out to earn extra money. Hiring out was a common practice. It meant that slaves could work for others, earning their own money at nights and on Sundays. They had to give their owner some of the money they made, but they were allowed to keep the rest. In Harriet's case, she owed Mr. Stewart a dollar a week. Any other money she raised in her spare time belonged to her.

This was just the incentive Harriet needed. Sometimes slaves were able to earn enough money to buy their freedom, and Harriet was determined to do this. She hardly sat still for a moment. On Sundays she hired herself out to clean up after large parties or to do gardening in nearby homes. Long into the night, she baked pies and took them to Bucktown to be sold in the market. She caught crabs in the muddy river flats and ran her own muskrat lines. There was hardly anything Harriet would not do to earn money, and soon the dried gourd she kept her pennies in was overflowing.

She buried the gourd in a hole under her bed and started filling up a second one. For the first time in her life, Harriet felt hopeful that things were going to work out for her. She knew how to make and save money, and she enjoyed the outdoor life working alongside her father. Ben taught her many things, including which berries and roots were good to eat, how to creep through a forest without even disturbing the birds, and how to tell the way north by studying the moss on tree trunks. Although they never talked about why Harriet might need such information, Harriet understood that her father was preparing her to find freedom one way or another.

The years slipped by, and eventually Harriet had saved forty dollars. She decided it was time to ask Dr. Thompson how much it would take for her to buy freedom. With shaking knees, she asked to see him one fine Sunday afternoon. She knew her body looked strong and healthy, but she walked with a limp and tried not to make herself look too valuable.

"I was wondering how much money it would take to buy my freedom," Harriet asked Dr. Thompson, keeping her gaze respectfully toward the floor. It would not do to look a white man in the eyes.

"Ha!" Dr. Thompson replied. "I hear you have become quite the worker, Harriet. Someone told me you can even drag a boat loaded with rocks down the river."

"Yes, sir," Harriet said, hating to be reminded of the times when Mr. Stewart made her perform tasks in front of his visitors so that he could show them how strong she was. He liked to hitch her to a boat loaded with stones and then order her to drag it behind her as she walked along the edge of the river. Such actions only made her feel like a performing animal. "So how much would my freedom cost?" she asked flatly.

"Five hundred!" Dr. Thompson snapped. "And that's not even saying I would have a mind to sell you. But if I did, I wouldn't take a penny less than five hundred dollars. You have years of good labor ahead of you."

Harriet tried hard to keep her expression passive. She would not give the doctor the satisfaction of seeing her crumble in front of him. "Very well," she replied. "Thank you for your time." With that she turned and fled.

Harriet ran for a long time, trying to outrun the knowledge that she was worth five hundred dollars to her owner. What could she do now? It would take a lifetime to earn that kind of money.

Slowly the reality that she might spend the rest of her life as a slave settled over Harriet. She often toyed with the idea of running away. After all, she knew which way was north, and her father had taught her how to survive in the wild. But the thought of her sudden bouts of sleeping kept her from taking the journey. Over half the slaves who tried to escape were caught, and these were slaves who did not fall asleep without a moment's notice. Harriet decided such a trip was just too dangerous for her. All she needed was to have a sleeping spell beside a busy road or when she was trying to cross a field, and she would be caught and sold south.

With her life stretching out in front of her as a continual round of labor, Harriet looked around for some way to make life more bearable.

Although she was now twenty-four years old, Harriet had never been paired off with a male slave to produce children. She was the only slave girl she knew who had not been forced to "marry," and she assumed that this was because of her sleeping fits. Slave masters did not want to take responsibility for sickly children. This left Harriet in the unusual position of being able to choose whether and when she should marry. *Marry*, though, was not really the right word, but it was the word everyone used. There was, in fact, no way for a slave to be officially married. Marriage was a legal matter, and a slave had no legal rights. Instead, slaves did something they called "jump the broom" together, and then they lived with their partner until one of them was sold off to another plantation. Then, with no prospects of ever seeing each other again, their masters ordered them to "marry" someone else.

Harriet knew most of the slaves in the Dorchester County area, as well as the few free black men. One of these men was named John Tubman, and Harriet often found herself chatting with him as she delivered her pies to the market. John Tubman was a big, strong man with a ready laugh and the habit of whistling as he walked. He explained to Harriet that his owner had died, leaving him and his mother their freedom in his will. Soon John began hinting about Harriet marrying him. With all thoughts of fleeing northward gone, Harriet decided to take her chance at happiness. She agreed and soon jumped the broom with John.

John moved into Harriet's cabin while she continued working as a slave and making money on the side where she could. It did not take her long to realize that John Tubman was carefree in all areas of his life. He seldom bothered to look for a job, relying instead on Harriet's gourds filled with money to tide them over when food was scarce or when he needed new clothes. He made fun of Harriet as she labored over their wedding quilt long into the evening and told her she worked far too hard for a slave.

Harriet grew dismayed as her precious savings began to dwindle, but there was little she could do about it. She and John were married now, and besides, she doubted she would ever make enough money to buy her freedom.

As married life continued, terrifying nightmares troubled Harriet. She often dreamed that she was being marched south in a chain gang or that she was watching a tiny baby being torn from her arms and carried away. At first, when she awoke in a cold sweat, she would prod John awake and tell him about her dreams. But he was not interested. "You worry far too much," he would laugh. "Take one day at a time. You were not sold yesterday, and you probably won't be sold tomorrow either."

Harriet's heart began to harden a little as she listened to her husband's words. It chilled her to think that he did not care whether she was a slave or free and that he seemed to have little appreciation for the fact that her whole life, and his too, could be torn apart in an instant. So when a woman wearing a long, gray dress and a trim bonnet stopped to talk to Harriet one day, she did not breathe a word of it to John Tubman. But Harriet remembered everything the woman said and played it over in her own mind many times.

It had been just after spring planting, and Harriet had been working alone down in the corner plot by the road. A petite woman had driven by in a buggy and stopped when she saw Harriet. "What name has thee?" she had asked kindly.

Harriet knew immediately that the woman must be a Quaker, since everyone knew that Quakers were the only people who said thee and thou.

"Harriet Tubman, mistress," Harriet had replied shyly. She was not used to talking to white women alone.

"Thou shall not call me mistress," the woman had said. "I am made in the image of God just as much as thee is. I am no less or more of a person than thee."

Harriet didn't know what to say to this, so she just nodded.

"My name is not important to thee now," the woman continued, "but if thee ever needs a friend, Harriet Tubman, thee will find a true friend in me. I live at the crossroads in the farmhouse with the hollyhocks and the white picket fence. Does thee know it?"

"Yes," Harriet replied, realizing that she had passed the house many times and had even seen the woman feeding chickens in the side yard.

"Come to my door whenever thee will, and thee will receive a welcome and a helping hand."

Harriet looked up for a moment and right into the woman's soft, blue eyes. They were honest, caring eyes. Once again, at a loss for words, Harriet nodded.

The Quaker woman flicked the reins of her horse, and the buggy started off down the road. Harriet watched it until it was out of sight. Even though the conversation had been less than a minute long, Harriet had the strange feeling it would play an important part in her destiny.

Chapter 6

"We've Got to Go North!"

"The young master is dead, and Sally's heard we're all going to be sold south! Dr. Thompson said so," one of the houseboys yelled to Harriet as he ran toward the fields. "The big house is in an uproar." Harriet dropped the ax she was using to chop firewood and raced off to find her husband.

"John, John. The worst thing has happened!" she yelled as she threw open the door to their cabin.

John Tubman looked up from his place beside the fire. "Must be terrible!" he said jokingly.

"It is!" Harriet insisted. "The young master is dead, and Sally in the big house says she heard Dr. Thompson is gonna sell nearly all of us. Price of cotton's been droppin', and there's no reason any-more to keep us, since the young master's dead."

"You can't know that for sure," John said, easing his lanky frame off the floor. "I'm always telling you, Harriet, worrying will be the death of you."

"It's not about idle worrying this time, John," Harriet said. "This could be the end for us. I'm just a piece of property, remember. I could be sold south tomorrow."

"So what you gonna do about it? Run away?" John mocked.

Harriet whirled around and looked up at him. "I just might have to do that. What choice do I have?"

John grabbed Harriet by the wrist. She felt his fingers dig in. His voice turned to a cold snarl. "You run away, girl, and I'll report you to the doctor faster than you get to the property line. I'll let the dogs out to hunt you down myself if I have to. You belong here, and you ain't goin' nowhere. You hear me?"

Harriet clenched her teeth. "You let me go right now, John Tubman, or you will live to regret it," she said. He loosened his grip, and Harriet turned and walked out the door.

She took the long way to her parents' cabin so that there was less chance of her meeting anyone along the way. Tears were streaming down her face as she struggled to make sense of her husband's cruelty. How could she ever get through to John what a nightmare it was to belong to a slave owner? He just did not understand. He often asked Harriet what more she could want besides what she already had, and her answer was always the same—the freedom to make her own decisions, to decide when and where to work, and if she stayed put in one place, the freedom to travel around.

Harriet found three of her brothers—Henry, Jim, and John—gathered around the door of her parents' cabin.

"Ben's gone to fetch Old Rit from churning butter in the dairy," Henry told her. "When she hears about the master's death, it'll pitch her into a terrible fit. She'll have us separated and sold south in a instant."

"You heard what Sally's said?" Harriet asked.

"Yep," Henry replied.

"You think she's telling the truth?"

"Sure, she is," Jim replied. "She wouldn't make something like that up. Besides, the plantation's running down fast, and the doctor needs some cash to fix it up. Makes sense he'd sell off some property."

Harriet nodded. Somehow she had never gotten used to the idea that she was property that could be exchanged for cash if her master needed money. "We've got to go north!" she whispered desperately. "It's now or never."

Three pairs of eyes swung around and fixed themselves on Harriet. She took a deep breath and went on. "Look, I been thinking 'bout this for a long time. I know a white lady in Bucktown. She can put us on the Underground Railroad. It's our only chance. What we got to lose?"

There was a long silence as the young men looked at one another.

Harriet was desperate to convince them to save themselves. "I'm telling you," she said, "there's two things I got a right to, and those two things are death and liberty. I mean to get me one or the other. No one's gonna take me back alive. I'll fight for my liberty, and when the time comes for me to go, the Lord will let them kill me. But I ain't gonna stop until I've given every ounce of strength to get my liberty."

After another long pause, Henry spoke up. "You think we can do it?"

"'Course we can. Like I said, I've been thinkin' on this for a long while. I know how to survive out there better than any man I know."

"What about John Tubman?" Jim asked.

Harriet shook her head. "He got all the freedom he wants. I ain't gonna say a word to him, or Ben and Old Rit, and you don't either. You hear me?"

The three men nodded, and Harriet realized for the first time that they looked to her, their little sister, as their leader. She seized the opportunity. "Look here, Saturday night's the best time to leave. We eat dinner like normal, and as soon as we can slip away, we meet in the corn patch behind the forge. That way we won't be missed until work on Monday morning. Are you comin' with me?" Harriet looked from one man to the other.

"But what about your spells? You ain't gonna be any good if you fall down asleep. Then what would we do?" her brother John asked.

"Hide me in the bush and wait for me to wake up," she replied. "Spells don't last too long."

"Doesn't sound safe to me," John went on. "What if you take a spell when we're in public?"

"That's a risk we'll have to take," Harriet replied. What else could she say? It was possible that she could take a fit and risk everyone's freedom. "Look," she said, "nothin's perfect, but what choice do we have? We have to trust that the good Lord is with us."

"I suppose," Henry answered, though he did not sound convinced.

"Are you coming with me or not?" Harriet asked them.

One by one, each of her brothers nodded his head.

"Good," she said. "Bring whatever food you can find with you, and wrap some rags around you under your shirts to keep warm."

For the rest of the week, Harriet could think of nothing else but escape. John Tubman had used up all of her savings by now, but she did what she could to gather provisions for the journey. She salted down half a herring that John had caught and skimped on the flour when she made their supper cakes so that she could make an extra large one on Saturday night.

When Saturday night came, Harriet spread the ashes in the fire so that it died down faster than normal. Once the flames had grown weak, John lay down on the blankets and announced that it was time for bed. He motioned for Harriet to crawl in beside him. She did so, praying that her breath would stay even and he would not feel her heart beating erratically through her thin dress. Within minutes Harriet heard the even snoring of her husband. She waited another minute or so and then slipped silently from under the blanket.

She gathered the food into a bandana and folded the blanket over her husband. Then opening the door very carefully, she stepped into the brisk September air.

The moon was nearly full, and she had no difficulty finding her way to the forge. She crept among the cornstalks and then stood listening. Presently she heard a rustle and then another as her three brothers joined her.

"Ready?" Harriet asked.

"Yes," her brothers replied in unison.

"Follow me, then," Harriet said, moving eastward toward the forest. "We'll go through the forest to Bucktown. No sense in going near a road."

As they made their way along, the three brothers crashed through the forest behind Harriet. To Harriet's surprise, every hoot of an owl or sound of a squirrel scampering up a tree seemed to scare them.

Then, far off in the distance, Harriet heard the sound of a hound baying. Her brothers heard it too and stopped.

"They're after us!" Jim exclaimed. "I knew they would be."

"Don't be stupid," Harriet told him. "They don't know we're missing yet. We haven't even been away for an hour."

"Well, them patrollers are gonna be on our tails in no time. What we gonna do? Remember Old Barra who escaped. When Dr. Thompson found him, he hacked both his ears off with a rusty knife, then sold him south anyway," Jim continued.

"If I'm gonna be sold south, I'd rather be with two ears attached," Henry interjected. "Besides, once the doctor finds four of us have gone at once, there'll be no end of news about us. Handbills will be spread far and wide before Monday night, and every slave owner in the area will bring his dogs to join in the hunt for us. I don't know what we were thinking, letting you talk us into this fool of a scheme, Harriet. This ain't never gonna work. Let's get back on our own before we're dragged back behind a horse."

"Yeah, and who knows if we'd be any better off up north anyway," John said. "Never met anyone who made it there, have you?"

Harriet turned to stare at her brother, hardly able to believe what he was saying. "Of course we've never met anyone who's made it north. They're living free up there, and they ain't comin' back here to be captured. What's wrong with you all? Don't you want your rightful freedom?"

"Not if it costs me my life!" Jim exclaimed.

"Me neither," Henry agreed. "I'm going back. Better the devil you know than the devil you don't."

"Please don't," Harriet pleaded with them. "If you do, you'll die in a cotton field somewhere never havin' breathed the air of freedom. How could you even think of going back?"

"I ain't thinking about it. I'm doing it!" Henry announced as he turned around and began walking in the direction they had just come.

"Me too," Jim and John agreed.

"Well, I'm goin' on alone then," Harriet said defiantly.

"No, you're not," Henry said. "I'm not going to be the one telling the bad news to Old Rit that you're a runaway. You're coming back with us."

Harriet opened her mouth to protest, but before a word came out, all three of her brothers had grabbed her arms and legs and hauled her into the air. She kicked and fought for all she was worth, but even her strong body was no match for three grown men.

The next hour was the most frustrating and humiliating hour of Harriet's life. She could hardly believe that her brothers lacked the courage to run for freedom, since in all likelihood they were going to be sold south very soon. But there was nothing she could do about it. The three men dumped her unceremoniously outside her cabin, and as they disappeared into the darkness, Henry whispered, "Be grateful you're alive, girl."

Harriet slipped inside. John stirred. "Where you been?" he muttered half asleep.

"Just sitting on the doorstep looking at the stars," Harriet told him. "It's a beautiful night."

"Uh," John replied as he rolled over.

Harriet slipped back into bed beside her husband and thought about one particular star—the North Star. It beckoned her, and as she drifted off to sleep she made a promise to herself that she would follow the star, and soon.

The following Monday Harriet knew she had to leave. Sally had sent word with the water boy that there was a rumor that Harriet and three of her brothers had been sold and were due to be picked up by their new owner the next morning. Harriet kept bending and picking the corn as she digested the news. She would have to leave as soon as everyone went to bed and head straight for the Quaker woman's cottage. It was too late to imagine what might happen if she had one of her sleeping spells, but she had to leave, and she had no choice but to go alone.

The rest of the day dragged on, and Harriet was glad when the bell rang for the field hands to quit. As Harriet walked back from the fields, she ran into her mother, who was going to milk the cow. Her mother looked tired and defeated, and Harriet took the pail from her hand. "I'll milk Dot for you, Mama," she said gently. "You go make your dinner and get some rest."

Old Rit looked at Harriet with a grateful expression. "Don't know what I'd do without you, girl," she said.

Harriet turned away and started toward the milking shed. *One way or another, you're going to have to do without all of your children by tomorrow,* Harriet thought, feeling grateful she had no children of her own to cause her such sorrow.

Once the milking was done, Harriet carried the pail of milk to the kitchen near the big house and set it on the back step. Then she walked around the side of the house to the dining room. Her sister MaryAnn was setting the silverware on the table. Harriet ached to tell her that she was going, especially since she wanted her parents to know beyond any doubt that she had gone north.

But how could she communicate with MaryAnn? It was too risky to talk to her through the window, as Dr. Thompson would be coming in to dine at any moment. Suddenly Harriet thought of a song her father used to sing to her. She stood beside the open window and started to sing:

> I'm sorry I'm going to leave you,
> Farewell, oh farewell,
> But I'll meet you in the morning,
> Farewell, oh farewell.

Harriet watched keenly as her sister's expression changed. She knew that MaryAnn understood what she meant. She sang on.

> I'll meet you in the morning,
> I'm bound for the Promised Land,
> On the other side of Jordan,
> Bound for the Promised Land.
> I'll meet you in the morning,
> Safe in the Promised Land,
> On the other side of Jordan,
> Bound for the Promised Land.

When Harriet had finished, MaryAnn turned her head toward the window and nodded, tears streaming down her face. Harriet ran to her cabin, hardly daring to think about the enormous journey she was about to embark upon alone.

Once again Harriet waited until her husband was asleep before she slipped out into the darkness. This time it was much easier, without her brothers crashing through the underbrush behind her. She wondered why Ben had not taught any of them the ways of the forest as he had taught her. Harriet reassured herself that it was because she was destined to escape.

In almost no time at all, Harriet found herself standing in the shadow of a large oak tree looking at the cottage with the picket fence and the chicken run. Her heart thumped as she contemplated knocking on the door and asking for help. She recalled the woman's gentle, honest eyes and her words, "Come to my door whenever thee will, and thee will receive a welcome and a helping hand." Even so, it was an enormous step to trust a white woman. It was, in fact, something that Harriet had never done before. White people, even kind white people, stuck together to keep slaves in their place. It took every ounce of courage Harriet possessed to believe that this white woman would actually help her.

Harriet took a deep breath and stepped into the moonlight. She could see a lamp glowing in one of the rooms as she rapped gently on the door. The door swung open, and the Quaker woman stood in the doorway. As soon as the woman saw who it was, she grabbed Harriet's arm. "Come in quickly," she said.

Once they were inside, the woman poured Harriet a cup of milk. "Thee is in need of help?" she asked.

Harriet nodded. "I'm Harriet Tubman, and you told me to come to you any time of the day or night."

"Quite right," the Quaker woman agreed. "I remember thee well. Thee is from Dr. Thompson's place. What is it I can do for thee?"

Harriet took another deep breath, conscious that if this was a trick, she was about to fall headlong into it. "I need to board the railroad tonight. I have been sold south, and my new owner is due to pick me up in the morning."

"Thee was right to come," the Quaker woman said in a soothing voice. "It is not God's intention that one man should own another's soul. He will go with thee."

"What should I do?" Harriet asked.

The Quaker woman walked over to a desk and pulled out a piece of paper. "Can thee read?" she asked.

"No," Harriet replied. "No one ever showed me."

"Then thee must listen carefully," the woman said. "Thee cannot stay here tonight. Thy new master will be looking for thee by midmorning for sure. Speed is thy friend. Thee has over ninety miles to go to get to the North. Thee must cross the Mason-Dixon Line." She sat down beside Harriet and looked directly at her. "The Underground Railroad is not a real railroad. It is a series of places slaves like thyself will find food and shelter along the way north. I can direct thee to thy next stop. Thee must reach the Choptank River to the north. Thee knows it?"

"Yes," Harriet replied. "I have journeyed that far with my father when he went to sell logs down the river."

"Good," the Quaker woman said. "It is a long walk, close to thirty miles through the swamp and forest. Walk through as many streams as thee can. Bloodhounds cannot pick up thy scent in water. Once thee reaches the river, follow it northward toward its source. The river will become very narrow as thee journeys up it, and eventually thee will find it is merely a trickle. When thee can jump across it in one step, thee must leave it and follow the road to the left of it. It will take thee northeast to Camden, Delaware, a distance of about fifteen miles. Thee must hide during the day and journey at night. Just before thee gets to town, look for a white house with green shutters and a red brick chimney. Thee will find Friends there by the name of Hunn." She stopped, wrote a few words on the piece of paper, and handed it to Harriet. "When thee knocks on the door, someone will ask who goes there. Thee must reply, 'A friend in need.' Repeat that."

"A friend in need," Harriet repeated, fixing the phrase in her mind.

"That's right. Here, give this note to Ezekiel Hunn, and he will tell thee what to do next. Ezekiel is a true Friend to all who seek help." She took Harriet's callused hands in her own. "I shall be praying for thee until I hear thee has arrived safely north. Thee must go now, Harriet Tubman, and God shall go with thee."

Chapter 7

Guided by the North Star

Harriet trudged on through the trees and underbrush. Tendrils of wild grapevines and honeysuckle pulled at her hair, but she kept moving, guided by the North Star that peeked through the trees. Occasionally when she thought she heard something, she would dive into the underbrush for cover, where she would stay motionless until she felt that the danger had passed. On one occasion the danger turned out to be nothing but a rabbit hopping by. Another time it was four men on horseback on a nearby road, patrolling for runaway slaves. Harriet dared not breathe until the sound of the men had faded into the distance. From time to time an owl hooted somewhere above as if to beckon Harriet on to freedom.

Finally the North Star began to fade, and the first light of dawn spread across the Maryland countryside. Exhausted from walking all night, Harriet crawled into the underbrush and, after making sure she was fully concealed by foliage, went to sleep.

Several hours later she awoke with a start. She couldn't sleep now, no matter how tired she felt. Dr. Thompson was sure to know she had run away by now and would have sent out men and dogs to track her down. Harriet had to keep moving until she reached the Choptank River. Then she could walk in the river and, she hoped, throw the bloodhounds off her trail.

Now that she was traveling in daylight, Harriet had to be extra vigilant. She listened for any noise that might indicate that someone was nearby. Sometimes she got on her hands and knees and crawled through the underbrush so as not to be seen. Finally, after squelching through a bog, she could see the steep, muddy banks of the Choptank come into view. Soon Harriet pulled off her shoes, slid into the river, and began heading upstream. Sometimes she waded through water that was ankle deep, and at other times the water was waist deep or deeper. Finally she began to notice the river narrowing. By the time the North Star had climbed into the night sky to guide her again, the river was barely a trickle and she could hop across it in one step. It was time to find the road that ran nearby and begin following it.

Harriet eventually found the road. She cautiously began following it in a northeasterly direction, being careful to stay in the shadow of the scrubby bushes that lined its sides. Small farms were dotted along the road, and Harriet was sure to give them a wide berth as she passed so that no dogs would begin to bark and give away her presence to anyone inside.

Finally, after many hours of walking, Harriet reached a house that matched the description she had been given. However, since it was still dark, and since Harriet was suspicious of white people, she decided to wait until the sun came up so that she could further check out the house before knocking on the door. She made her way over to a pile of hay and slumped down beside it. No sooner had she sat down than her sleep-heavy eyelids began to close. But now was not the time for sleep. What if she slept past sunrise and someone discovered her hiding by the hay? Harriet clambered back onto her weary feet and made her way over to the barn. She walked back and forth next to the barn, trying to stay awake.

After what seemed like an eternity to Harriet, the sun began to climb above the eastern horizon and spread its web of golden rays across the Delaware countryside. Harriet watched the house closely, and about half an hour after sunrise, a woman emerged from the house and began to sweep the yard. When she was sure everything was safe, Harriet emerged from the shadows of the barn and walked over to the woman. She pulled the slip of paper she had been given from her pocket and handed it to the woman. The woman read it and then handed the broom to Harriet. "Here, sweep," she said.

As Harriet began to sweep the yard, the woman disappeared inside the house. Harriet waited anxiously to see what would happen next, planning an escape route if this was the wrong house and she had to flee. Time seemed almost to stop as Harriet swept and waited. But as she thought about the situation, she began to feel herself relax. Why else would the woman have given her the broom? Only so that anyone passing by on their way to Camden would think Harriet was a house slave and not a runaway from Maryland.

After several minutes a man stepped out of the house. He was dressed in dark clothes and wore a wide-brimmed hat. Harriet recognized it as the dress of a Quaker, and she let out a deep sigh of relief. The man strode over to her.

"Good morning to thee," the man said pleasantly. "I am Ezekiel Hunn. Please come inside."

Inside the house Harriet was introduced to Ezekiel Hunn's wife, and then she sat down to a hearty breakfast of eggs and pork and corn cakes. Following breakfast she was shown to a bedroom, where she climbed into a bed. It was the first bed Harriet had ever slept in, and she marveled at how soft it was. She sank into the feather mattress and was soon sound asleep. It was midafternoon before she awoke and reluctantly climbed out of the wonderful bed that had made her feel as though she were sleeping on a cloud.

"After dark," Ezekiel told her, "I will take thee in the wagon to the edge of Smyrna so that I am home by dawn and no one will notice my absence. From there thee must make thy way to Middletown before sunrise. My brother John will give thee shelter when thee arrives."

Harriet nodded, and soon after sunset she climbed into the back of Ezekiel's wagon. She lay still in the bottom as Ezekiel pulled a tarpaulin over her to hide her. After several hours of bone-jarring travel, the wagon came to a halt. Harriet heard Ezekiel tell her it was time to climb out from under the tarpaulin.

"Follow this road quickly, and it will take thee to Middletown." Before turning his wagon around, Ezekiel explained to Harriet how to get to his brother's house and what the house looked like. "God go with thee and keep thee safe," he said as he cracked the reins for the horses to begin the journey home.

"Thank you, sir," Harriet replied. She wanted to say more, but she didn't know how. It was such a strange realization that there were white people in the South willing to risk their lives to help slaves escape to freedom.

As Ezekiel had said, the road took Harriet straight to his brother's house at the edge of Middletown. Harriet arrived just before sunrise and was quickly whisked inside, where once again she ate a hearty breakfast and slept in a soft bed.

"From here thee must travel on to Wilmington,"

John Hunn told Harriet when she awoke. "In Wilmington, Thomas Garrett is expecting thee. He will help thee on the next leg of thy journey. Alas, I cannot take thee there. If Friend Garrett and I were to be seen together, suspicions would be raised, putting thee at risk."

Harriet nodded.

"I will take thee by carriage to the outskirts of town, and from there thee must walk alone. When thee comes to the first bridge to Wilmington, go to the graveyard upon the hill overlooking it. Hide among the headstones until a man comes. He will say to thee, 'I bring a ticket for the railroad.' Go with him, and he shall lead thee over the bridge into the town."

For the first few miles of her journey to Wilmington, Harriet rode with John Hunn in his carriage, until he finally guided his horse to a halt at the side of the road.

"Thee must go on alone," John said to Harriet. "Take great care as thee travels. Many slaves travel this road, and there is already a reward out for thy capture. Be sure that thee stays in the shadows."

As she had done with his brother, Harriet thanked John Hunn for his help and kindness before she turned and headed into the darkness.

The North Star shone brightly above once more as Harriet moved in and out among the trees and the shadows at the edge of the road. She had walked for several miles, alert to any noise or movement in the distance, when she fell into one of her sleeping spells and slumped against a tree.

Harriet was unsure how long she had been asleep when she was startled awake by the sound of approaching horses. She froze in the shadow of the tree and peered out into the darkness. Three slave catchers rode up and stopped only a few feet from where she was hiding. She gripped the tree and held herself motionless, barely daring to breathe. She worried that her pounding heart would give her away.

"She can't have got farther than this," a voice said gruffly from atop one of the horses.

"Hunn's carriage was spotted earlier tonight south of here, but I can't believe she would have come this far. Perhaps we should double back and see if we can't spot her farther back down the road," another voice said.

"It's so dark, we can't see our fingers in front of us. I say we let the devil take her," the third voice said.

"Perhaps you're right," the gruff voice said before jerking the reins and wheeling his horse around. With a shout he galloped off in the direction from which he had come. The other two men quickly followed.

Harriet let out a deep breath and relaxed her rigid body. Slowly the pounding of her heart began to subside, and she started making her way along the road again.

Just as John Hunn had said, there was a cemetery on the hill above the first bridge that crossed into Wilmington. The bridge lay under the watchful eyes of slave catchers waiting to pounce on any wayward runaway slave who tried to cross over into the city. Since there was no way Harriet could make it across on her own, she crept up the rise to the graveyard. Wisps of fog had blown in from the river and floated around the gravestones, casting an eerie pall over the cemetery. But Harriet's desire for freedom pushed her forward. She crouched and crawled among the headstones trying to stay out of view while searching for the man she was to meet.

Minutes passed, and Harriet began to wonder whether the man was coming or, perhaps worse, had already come and, not finding her, had left. After all, she had no idea how long she had slept when she had her sleeping fit. Lost in her own gloomy thoughts, Harriet was oblivious to the footsteps approaching her from behind. Suddenly she felt a firm hand grab her shoulder. Harriet's heart beat so hard, it felt like it would burst out of her chest. She fought back the urge to scream as she swung around. A tall man stood in front of her.

"I bring a ticket for the railroad," the man whispered.

Harriet relaxed. "Thank you," she said. "You're here!"

"Put these on," the man said as he handed her a set of men's workclothes.

Harriet pulled on the shirt and the worn coveralls. She put a hat on her head, pushing her hair up inside and arranging it so that it covered the indentation and scar on the side of her head. When she had dressed, the man handed her a rake. Harriet looked just like a male worker.

When the sun arose, Harriet accompanied the man across the bridge into Wilmington. To anyone who passed them, they looked like a slave accompanying his master into town for a day's work.

Once they were in Wilmington, the man pointed the way to Thomas Garrett's house. He then quickly disappeared as Harriet rapped on the door. The door swung open, and Harriet was hustled inside, where Thomas Garrett greeted her.

"I am Harriet Tubman," Harriet introduced herself.

"Yes, I have been expecting thee," Thomas said. "Quickly now, follow me."

Thomas led Harriet up a flight of steps and stopped in front of a bookcase. He pulled out two books and reached to the back of the shelf to turn a latch. The bookcase swung back to reveal a secret room. "Welcome to the waiting room of the Underground Railroad," he announced.

Harriet stepped into the room.

"Only close friends know of the existence of this room. Thee will be safe in here. But thee must be quiet—my shoe factory is directly below," Thomas said. "I will visit thee a little later." With that he heaved the bookcase closed, shutting Harriet in the room.

For two days Harriet stayed in the room. Thomas visited several times a day, bringing food and other items to make her stay in the confined quarters as comfortable as possible. Then early on Sunday morning, six days after Harriet had run away from the plantation in Maryland, Thomas entered the room carrying some clean clothes, a black veil, and a new pair of shoes.

"Put these on," Thomas said. "When the people of town are in church this morning, thee will leave town with me in my carriage."

Harriet hurriedly put on the new shoes and clean clothes and draped the veil over herself. An hour later Thomas guided her out to his carriage. Harriet sat next to him in the front of the carriage, the veil hiding her features so that she looked like a lady out for a leisurely ride in the country with her host.

About two miles outside of Wilmington, Thomas pulled the carriage to a halt. "Take that path over there," he said, pointing to a well-worn track that led away from the road they were on. "Walk for an hour and thee will come to a highway. Nearby thee will see a sign that marks the line between Delaware and Pennsylvania. Walk past the sign, and thee will be free! Here, I have written Pennsylvania on this piece of paper. Compare it to the sign to be sure it is the right sign." He handed Harriet the piece of paper. "And here, take this too." He pressed a silver dollar into her hand. "Godspeed thee, Harriet Tubman."

"Thank you, sir, and may God bless you for all your help to me." With that Harriet climbed down from the carriage and headed off along the path. The new shoes Thomas had given her felt wonderful on her feet. He had told Harriet that he gave a new pair of shoes to every escaping slave he helped.

Finally the track led to a highway. Cautiously

Harriet looked around to make sure no one was about before she stepped out from behind a bush onto the highway. She took several steps north, then noticed a signpost about one hundred yards in the distance. She began to run to get to it as fast as possible.

Harriet drew a deep breath when she reached the signpost. She pulled out the piece of paper Thomas had given her and held it up to the sign. The letters matched. She let out a whoop of joy and stretched out her arms as wide as she could before taking a big step. And with that step she crossed the Mason-Dixon Line. She drew another deep breath and filled her lungs with air—free air breathed by a free woman in a free land!

Next Harriet studied her hands. For the first time in her life, they, along with the rest of her body, belonged to her! No one would ever be able to sell her or whip her again. She looked around. Everything was strangely different from how it had appeared just a few moments ago. The sun cast a golden hue on the sky, the trees were somehow more majestic, and the fields were wide and welcoming.

"I think I'm in heaven!" Harriet told herself as she continued to walk north along the road. She winced as a buggy drove past. She forced herself to stay in clear view instead of ducking for cover in some nearby bushes. "I am free now, and no one can touch me," she reassured herself. "I'm never going south again."

Harriet continued to walk on late into the afternoon. She still hadn't reached Philadelphia, but judging by how busy the road was, she decided she must be close. Many of the people she passed on the road were black, and at first Harriet scrutinized their faces searching for someone she might recognize from Maryland. But each time she found herself staring into the face of a stranger. Slowly Harriet's joy at being free began to give way to an intense loneliness. She had been so focused on escaping north that she had not had time to think about her mother and father and brothers and sisters back home. Now freedom seemed strangely empty without someone to share it with. And the more Harriet walked, the more she realized that her family mattered more to her than anything else in the world. She could not enjoy her freedom until they were free as well.

But how could they all be free? As Harriet puzzled over this question, she thought of her brother John's words to her when they had given up their first escape attempt. "Yeah, and who knows if we'd be any better off up north anyway?" he had said. "Never met anyone who made it there, have you?" John's words became a challenge to Harriet. She was north, and she was free, and she vowed to herself that she would find a way to go back across the Mason-Dixon Line and lead her family to freedom. It was not a vow she made rashly, nor was it one she would be able to fulfill straightaway. Harriet would need a plan, money, and friends to help her in her new mission.

Now the road did not seem so lonely. The thought that one day she would be walking it with members of her family cheered Harriet on, and by nightfall she had reached the outskirts of Philadelphia. She found an old shed to spend the night in. Before she went to sleep, Harriet fingered the silver dollar Thomas had given her. She promised herself that it would be the first of many dollars she would save, which in turn would finance her plan to lead her family to freedom.

The following morning Harriet set about finding a job. Since she had been hired out so many times as a slave, she knew how to do a variety of things. She found a woman who wanted someone to scrub down her walls and floors, and although Harriet never liked housework, she took the job gladly. Her efforts were rewarded with two more dollars at the end of the week. As Harriet dropped the two coins into her pocket, she listened to them jangle. It was the first money she had ever earned where she could keep it all. She felt exhilarated.

After cleaning the walls and floors, Harriet moved on down the street, knocking on back doors and asking if anyone had work that needed to be done. Sometimes she took a job for an hour, sometimes for a day or a week but never for very long. Harriet enjoyed the novelty of being able to change jobs whenever she felt like it!

Before long she had earned quite a bit of money, and she saved all of it except the small amount she spent on food and lodging. Finally, by December she had enough money saved to purchase the first item she needed for her plan to go south and rescue her family from slavery. She stepped into a pawnshop on bustling Chestnut Street and pointed to the heavy silver pistol in the window. "How accurate is that?" she asked.

The merchant raised his eyebrows a little, but he picked the pistol up and put it on the counter. "All depends on the shooter," he said. "You looking for something for yourself?"

"Yes," Harriet replied. "And if it is a reliable shot, I'd be much obliged if you could show me how to use it."

The merchant showed her how and where to load the bullets, how to cock the gun, and how to aim and fire it.

Harriet left the pawnshop with the pistol in her bag, shaking her head once again at how different the North was from the South. In Maryland it had been illegal for a black person to own any firearm. "Too worried we'd all turn out like Nat Turner," Harriet told herself as she fingered the gun in her bag. "I can't wait to tell William Still what I've bought. Maybe now he'll believe I'm serious."

Harriet hurried back to her cooking job at a nearby hotel, and later that evening she met her new friend William Still in the park. William was secretary of the Pennsylvania Anti-Slavery Society, and one of the hotel workers had introduced them to each other. William took Harriet's arm, and they strolled together around the fountain and manicured lawns.

"I have a pistol now," Harriet told him.

William groaned. "Harriet," he said gently, "how many times do I have to tell you, it's not going to work out for you to go south. It is dangerous. Don't you see?"

"What does danger mean to me?" she retorted. "There's no use in me having freedom if I can't share it with my family."

"It's just not possible," William continued firmly. "There are only two types of people we use as conductors on the Underground Railroad—white people—Quakers and other abolitionists—and free black men with papers to prove it. The South is no place for someone who is still listed as a runaway slave and, as I have pointed out before, no place for a woman! Some of the Quaker women help out from time to time, but we don't have a single black woman conductor, and I like you too much to make you our first." He stopped and looked pleadingly into Harriet's eyes. "Look, there are men traveling to the Eastern Shore. We will get one of them to ask about what has happened to your family."

Harriet stared back at him defiantly. "I may be a woman," she said, drawing herself up to her full five feet in height, "but no one ever took that into consideration when I had to split half a cord of wood a day or get hitched up to a mule at plowing time. No, sir, no one ever said, 'Lookie here, that woman can't do that!' Now for the first time ever my life's mine to live and die as I please. And I'm here to tell you, Mr. William Still, that you ain't gonna be the first man since freedom to tell Harriet Tubman what she can and cannot do!"

William sighed. "You're one of a kind! At least promise me one thing. You will bide your time and talk to me before you run off and do anything foolhardy."

"Agreed," Harriet replied grudgingly. "But you ain't gonna talk me out of it, you can be sure of that."

"And in the meantime I'll see what we can find out about where your family is and who owns them now."

"Fine," Harriet said. "The more information we have, the better we can plan. Right?"

William smiled down at Harriet. "Whatever you say," he agreed.

Chapter 8

Time to Conduct Her Passengers

Harriet tried her best to concentrate on washing the dishes at the hotel where she was working, though her hands shook so much she could barely trust herself not to break the crockery. After she had finished the dishes, she scrubbed the floor and laid the tables for breakfast the next morning. As she worked, the doorman's words rang in her ears. "Ain't none of us safe now. President Fillmore signed the compromise into law. I'm telling you, ain't none of us safe now!"

Harriet worked as fast as she could so that she could escape her job and run down to see William at the Anti-Slavery Society. "No sense in getting all worried about it," she told herself. "William will be able to tell me what this law is all about."

As soon as she had finished her work for the day, Harriet untied her apron, hung it on the hook at the back door, and ran down the street. She arrived at the Anti-Slavery Society to discover that many other free blacks had the same idea. A large crowd had gathered at the doorway. Inside Harriet could make out William, standing on a table and waving a newspaper and yelling to the crowd.

Harriet pushed her way forward to hear what he was saying.

"As many of you know," William said, "until now the United States has consisted of fifteen states that allow slavery and fifteen that do not. Today that balance has been upset. California has been accepted into the union as a state in which slavery is not allowed, and the land won in the Mexican war has been divided into two new territories, New Mexico and Utah. These two territories will not have federal restrictions on them. They can choose whether they will be free or slave territories, and the slave trade is to be abolished in the District of Columbia."

A cheer went up from the crowd, though Harriet did not join in. She was still trying to understand what this all meant.

William held up his hands and continued. "All is not well, though, my friends. While trading slaves has been abolished in our capital, owning slaves has not, and dark clouds are forming over our own so-called free state of Pennsylvania."

A hush fell over the crowd as people strained to catch every word.

"I am, unfortunately, speaking of the last provision of the compromise bill. It is the Fugitive Slave Act, and it states that any slave who runs away is, in fact, stealing his master's property and that his master has the right to have that property returned. The law gives slave owners the right to pursue their slaves into free states and drag them back to slavery. Such a slave does not have the right to be heard in court. His only recourse is to a special commissioner, who has the sole power to decide the matter of freedom or slavery for anyone accused of being a runaway. To make matters worse, the law allows for the commissioner to be paid five dollars if he frees the black man, and ten if he sides with the slave owner and sends him back to a life of slavery."

William paused for a long moment, but no one spoke. Then he continued. "What is more, all citizens can be called upon by the sheriff to help capture a wanted black man, woman, or child. If they refuse to give such help, this new law says they can be fined and sent to prison."

Harriet felt the blood drain from her face, and she steadied herself against the woman standing beside her. *So the doorman's words had been true,* she thought bitterly. *Ain't none of us safe now.* Indeed, if her master decided to send someone after her, she could be collared and chained and sent south again despite the fact that she was living in free Pennsylvania.

As Harriet lay in bed that night, she thought about this new Compromise of 1850, as the law was being called. It all seemed so wrong. She was a human being, not a piece of property to be hunted down and returned to her "owner." Southern politicians were simply wrong. The thirty thousand fugitive slaves living in the North were not valued at fifteen million dollars, or any other figure for that matter. It was wrong to put a figure—any figure—on a human life. Harriet felt chilled at the thought of her family members standing on an auction block while white men bid for them.

Harriet assured herself that although this new bill might work for a while, in the end it would fall apart. According to the politicians, it was supposed to end the questions about slavery once and for all, but to Harriet it only served to stir things up. Surely in the end Northerners would not take kindly to wealthy Southern gentlemen hunting for human beings in their towns and cities. But what would Harriet do in the meantime? As she thought about this, her countenance suddenly brightened. William had stalled her from going south to get her family because she would be putting her life in danger. But now, as a runaway slave, her life was in danger anywhere in the United States, so there was nothing to stop her from going south! Harriet hardly slept the rest of the night. Somehow the need to gather her family around her seemed more urgent than ever. She promised herself that tomorrow she would find out whether there was any news about them.

The following evening a crowd was still gathered outside the Anti-Slavery Society office, but Harriet was able to make her way inside and soon found herself face-to-face with her friend William. "Do you have any news of my family?" she asked.

William nodded. "Come into my office where it's quiet," he said, guiding Harriet by the arm. Her heart beat fast as she wondered what the news might be. Were her parents still alive? Had her husband decided to come north after all? Were her brothers and sisters safe? Her mind ran wild with the possibilities.

"I received a letter from a friend in Maryland just this morning concerning your sister MaryAnn. She has a two-year-old boy and a new baby."

Harriet nodded. MaryAnn had married a freeman named John Bowley and had a son by him. But now she had another baby. Harriet wondered whether it was a boy or a girl.

"Sadly," William continued, "my contacts tell me that MaryAnn and the children are to be sold at auction at the end of the month."

Harriet's hands flew to her face. "No," she gasped. "I have to get to them before they are separated and gone forever."

William patted Harriet on the arm. "I know what you are feeling, but we have some people who can help MaryAnn and the children get as far as Baltimore. Everything has changed since the Fugitive Slave Act passed, and it will be more dangerous than ever to go south. But if you feel you must, we will need someone to lead them from Baltimore north. Think about it tonight, and tell me tomorrow if you are willing to risk your life for your sister."

Harriet gulped back the tears. "I don't need to think about it for another moment. I have spent every hour of my freedom working and saving so I could rescue my family. Of course I'll go to MaryAnn."

Three days later Harriet sat in a spacious kitchen in Baltimore, Maryland. She was in the home of a rich Quaker family, waiting for MaryAnn and her family to arrive. As she waited, her stomach twisted into knots. She had no idea how the Underground Railroad planned to spirit MaryAnn, John, and the children away, or whether they had even been successful at doing this. Her apprehension grew along with the lengthening shadows of the afternoon sun. A million questions tormented her. Did their conductor know how to drug the babies with opium so that they would not cry? Did MaryAnn have the courage to go through with the plan, whatever it entailed? And what if John was caught with MaryAnn and the children? Would he be hanged on the spot as an example to other free blacks who dared think of rescuing slave relatives?

"Thee must put thy trust in God and not waste thy strength with fretting," the woman of the house said.

"I know," Harriet sighed. "I do trust in God, but it's the waiting that is so difficult. If I had something to do, I'd feel much better."

The woman laughed. "If it's work that would put thee at ease, Harriet, there is plenty of that about. Sit down here, and thee and I shall slice green beans for tomorrow."

Harriet sat at the table and picked up a knife, glad to have something to occupy her thoughts. She had sliced only a few beans into a bowl when she heard a faint tap at the door. She looked at the woman, who motioned her to open the door. Harriet raced over and opened it. Standing in front of her were MaryAnn and John. Both of them cradled a sleeping child in their arms!

Harriet rushed forward and hugged her sister.

"Get thee inside and close the door before someone sees thee," the woman of the house demanded.

In a moment Harriet snapped back to attention and hurried the family inside. With them were three young men Harriet assumed were also runaways. As the door closed, a smell of onions settled over the room.

"Come and sit by the oven," Harriet said, taking the baby from MaryAnn's arms. "It's a boy?"

MaryAnn nodded.

"He's so beautiful. What's his name?" Harriet asked.

"Harkless," MaryAnn replied, grinning from ear to ear. "He won't wake up for a while yet. We had to drug him to keep him from crying."

Harriet nodded her approval. "Now tell me all about your escape."

The mistress of the house made hot coffee for the group and fed them thickly buttered bread and cheese. Between mouthfuls MaryAnn and John told Harriet their story.

Things had moved so quickly that MaryAnn and the two children were already being held in pens at the courthouse in Cambridge where the slave auction was to be held. A Quaker man who was part of the Underground Railroad had come up with a daring plan to save them. It required John Bowley to have nerves of steel. The Quaker man wrote an official-looking letter asking the court warden to release MaryAnn and the children into John's custody, explaining that John was a trusted servant who was to bring the three of them to their master. According to the letter, the master had a potential buyer for the slaves at the hotel where he was dining.

John delivered the letter to the warden, and he had been so convincing that the warden unlocked the pen MaryAnn and the children were in and told them to follow John. Of course, MaryAnn desperately wanted to ask John what was going on, but she played her part well and hushed her older son before he could call John "Pappy."

The little family walked slowly down the street, trying not to draw any attention to themselves. It took all of their effort not to burst into a run. Finally they reached the corner. John looked around. Since no one appeared to be watching them, he darted into an alley between two houses. "Quick, follow me," he urged MaryAnn.

Once he had checked that the way was clear, John led his family to the back of one of the houses and in through the unlocked back door. A Quaker woman was waiting for them and led them to the attic, where they stayed for the rest of the day. Once it got dark, they were brought downstairs and fed before being bundled onto the floor of a farmer's wagon. Sacks were thrown over them, and they began the long journey north, including more wagon rides, this time amid piles of potatoes and onions, and a midnight sailing up the Chesapeake Bay before they arrived in Baltimore.

"And we are only halfway there," Harriet told her sister and brother-in-law.

"But I know we'll make it with you beside us, Harriet!" MaryAnn exclaimed. "Tell us, what's it like to be free?"

Harriet and her sister sat talking for a long time about what had happened in both of their lives since Harriet had run away more than twelve months before. That night—and the five nights after that, as everyone prepared for the second half of the journey to freedom—Harriet slept soundly.

Finally, nearly a week after they had been reunited, the all clear was given, and it was time for Harriet to conduct her "passengers" to the station at the end of the Underground Railroad. Harriet felt nervous as she set out with the group, but she dared not show her feelings. From now on she was the one everyone would look to in moments of crisis, and she steeled herself to be ready for anything that happened.

Traveling by night, Harriet led the group of runaway slaves north. They trudged through forests and across swamps. Early each morning they would arrive at the next station on the Underground Railroad, where they were hidden until night fell, at which time they again made their way north.

Finally, as Harriet had done more than a year before, the group crossed into Pennsylvania and then walked on to Philadelphia. Harriet had succeeded in fulfilling at least part of her vow. She had led her sister, along with her sister's husband and children, to freedom. But Harriet's mother and father and brothers still remained slaves in Maryland, and she would not rest until she had also led them to freedom.

Chapter 9

Moses

It was early spring 1851 when Harriet decided to go south again to guide her brother James to freedom. Snow still lay in places on the ground as she made her way through Delaware and on into northern Maryland, where James was enslaved on a plantation. She soon located her brother and two of his friends who also wanted to escape north. They started out after the sun had set, but an overseer saw them leave. Within minutes hounds were barking on their trail. Harriet guided the three men as fast as she could to the nearest river.

"We need to cross now!" she exclaimed, but the three men stood motionless. Fear of the dogs approaching from behind and the icy cold river they must cross was etched in their faces.

Harriet plunged on ahead. Soon the river was lapping at her chin, but she kept going. Finally she reached the far bank and climbed out. She motioned to the three men on the other side still paralyzed by fear. Finally, as the barking of the hounds got louder, James walked into the water. The other two men followed him, and eventually they made it across the river without a moment to spare.

The group raced on, and it wasn't until they had forded another river that the bloodhounds finally lost their scent. As dawn approached, Harriet led them all to a safe house on the Underground Railroad. Three days later she guided the three runaways into Pennsylvania and freedom.

Upon her return to Philadelphia, Harriet realized she could not stay there indefinitely. It was simply too dangerous to be a fugitive slave in the United States now that the tough fugitive slave law had been enacted. Although she was willing to risk her life going south to rescue her family, Harriet found it impossible to live with the daily, stomach-churning notion that she might be grabbed and chained up at any moment. Like so many other former slaves, she looked north to Canada.

Canada was part of the British Empire, and eighteen years earlier, in 1833, Queen Victoria had declared an end to slavery there. Once an American black slave reached the "paw of the British Lion," as Harriet called Canada, he or she was safe from ever being enslaved again. It was an easy decision for Harriet to make the move to St. Catharines on the Canadian side of Niagara Falls.

Just across the border from the United States, St. Catharines was a hotbed of activity for the American antislavery movement. Many of the town's six thousand residents were former slaves, determined to make a better life for themselves and their children. Many black and white leaders kept a close watch on what happened in St. Catharines, hoping it would either be a dismal failure or a glorious success, depending upon their view of slavery.

Harriet was relieved that her new home finally gave her and the other family members she hoped to rescue a safe place to live.

During this time Harriet also thought a lot about John Tubman. Often she rehearsed in her head what she would say to him when she finally saw him again. Surely, she told herself, the promise of a better life where everyone was free would entice him to follow her north, and they could be a family again. There might even be children!

The time soon came for her find out for sure. In the autumn of 1851, Harriet once again made her way back to Dorchester County, Maryland. On this trip south she decided to disguise herself as a man. She wore pants and a jacket and a felt hat pulled low on her brow to cover the telltale dent on the side of her head. About eleven o'clock on a bright moonlit night, Harriet sneaked around to the back of the old cabin she had shared with John and quietly tapped on the door. The door flung open, and there stood John, just as tall and handsome as ever. Harriet stepped forward and flung out her arms. "John!" she exclaimed. "I've come back for you."

"Who is it?" came a sleepy voice from inside.

"I don't know," John replied.

Harriet stepped into the cabin and in the light of a single candle saw another woman. She stepped back, hardly knowing what to say. "John, it's me, Harriet...your wife," she stuttered.

John lifted her chin and squinted as he looked at her. "Well, I'll be darned if it ain't you, all right," he replied coldly. "A bit late comin' home, ain't you—like maybe two years too late."

"She the one you told me about that ran off?" came the other woman's voice.

"The very one, Caroline," John replied. "But she ain't staying. There ain't no way I'm gonna go anywhere with her."

"But, John," Harriet began, hating the begging tone she heard in her voice. "I'm your wife. I've risked my life to come back for you. I live in Canada now, where everyone is free. Don't you want to be truly free with me?"

John laughed cruelly. "You never did get it, did you, Harriet? I am free, and I always will be free. You're the one who was the slave. Took the whole thing much too seriously for your own good, too."

Harriet looked desperately from John to Caroline, but she could see it was too late. John Tubman had another woman, and he had no intention of risking anything to accompany her north. Still, Harriet took a deep breath and spoke deliberately. "John, I'm giving you one last chance. Do you want to come north with me or not?"

"Get her out of here," Caroline interjected. "No one asked her to come."

John put his hands firmly on Harriet's shoulders and turned her around. Harriet staggered out the door and heard it close firmly behind her. She stumbled into a toolshed, trying to make sense of what had just happened. All of her dreams of making a happy family with John Tubman in St. Catharines were gone. She was now alone in the world.

As she sat among the hoes and the shovels in the toolshed, Harriet wondered what she should do next. Her plan had always been to rescue her own relatives and guide them to freedom, but what about the other slaves on the plantations she visited? Didn't they deserve a chance at freedom, too?

By the time it was midnight, Harriet had made up her mind. If John Tubman would not go with her, she would give his "seat" on the Underground Railroad to someone else! It was not about her and her family anymore—it was about taking anyone brave enough to follow her northward.

Harriet knew she had to act fast. In the morning John—or more likely, Caroline—might well tell an overseer that she was back in the area. Harriet had to round up anyone who wanted to escape north and get moving before dawn. She crept to the slave quarters and went from cabin to cabin asking if anyone wanted to go north with her.

Soon ten men and a single woman were hiding in the nearby woods waiting for Harriet to lead them away from the plantation.

Gathering the group together, Harriet began the long trek to the nearest station on the Underground Railroad. She tried not to think about John Tubman. *That part of my life is behind me now,* she thought to herself. *I have many more slaves to lead out of Egypt and into the Promised Land.*

The entire group made it to Canada in record time, just ahead of an unexpected cold snap.

Back in St. Catharines, Harriet took into her little house as many former slaves as she could. It took all of her energy and money to feed and clothe them and keep them warm. Slowly these runaways adjusted to their freedom and began looking for jobs.

Later that spring Harriet moved south to Cape May, New Jersey. Although she knew it was dangerous to leave Canada, she also knew she could make more money south of the border, and more money meant more people she could lead to freedom.

Harriet made several more trips as a conductor on the Underground Railroad, guiding about twenty more slaves to Canada. By then she knew the "Eastern Line" so well that people started to call her Moses. Harriet did not know what to think of such a grand title, but she was grateful for one thing—it was a man's name, and she hoped that it would confuse any slave owners trying to work out who it was who had "stolen" their property.

It was not until late fall 1854 that Harriet had the chance to rescue more members of her family. She had heard that three of her brothers, Benjamin, Henry, and Robert, were all in danger of being sold south. Benjamin and Robert had been transferred to another of Dr. Thompson's properties, forty miles north in Caroline County. Harriet's parents and Henry were still working on the original plantation.

It was difficult to get a message to her brothers, since none of them could read or write, but Harriet devised a clever plan. She asked a friend in Canada to write a letter to a free black man in Dorchester County whom she knew well. His name was Jacob Jackson, and he could be trusted to get a message to her brothers. There was just one problem. Harriet knew that slave owners watched Jacob's mail because they suspected him of helping slaves escape. She would have to think of a way to write him a letter that only he could understand.

In the end Harriet dictated what she wanted to say. She started off with some general words about the weather and then said, "Read my letter to the old folks, and give my love to them, and tell my brothers to be always watching unto prayer, and when the good old ship of Zion comes along, be ready to step aboard." The letter was signed "William Henry Jackson," the name of Jacob's son who lived in the North. Harriet knew that Jacob Jackson would guess that the letter was not really from his son, since William Henry had no brothers. She hoped that words like *good old ship of Zion* and *step onboard* would let Jacob know that "Moses" had really written the letter. A week later Harriet sent another coded letter telling her brothers to meet her near her parents' cabin on Christmas Eve.

As Harriet secretly made her way south, she thought about her parents. It was now five years since she had last seen them, and she longed to talk with them and find out how they were. But that was the problem. If Harriet did show up on their doorstep, she knew her father, Ben, would remain calm and in control of his emotions, but what about her mother? Old Rit had always been an emotional woman, wailing and praising the Lord in a loud voice. Could she be trusted not to make a scene, especially when she found out that Harriet had come to take three more of her sons away?

Eventually Harriet decided it was too big a gamble. Even though she would probably be within feet of her mother, Harriet knew it would be unwise to let her know she was there. Keeping her distance from Old Rit would be one of the greatest challenges Harriet ever faced.

It was raining hard on Christmas Eve, and Harriet was glad to find shelter in a fodder shed near the slave quarters. She peeked out through the slats and was rewarded with the sight of her father carrying firewood to the cabin. Harriet's heart thumped when she saw him, and everything in her wanted to rush out and into his arms. But she dared not go.

Soon two of her brothers, Benjamin and Robert, crept into the fodder shed.

"We're mighty glad to see you!" Benjamin exclaimed. "Jacob Jackson passed on the message to us, and we hoped we got it right."

"That you did!" Harriet replied, hugging first one, then the other of her brothers. "Now all we need is Henry."

"Hope he shows up soon," Robert said.

"I hope so, too. We don't have a lot of time to spare," Harriet said. "We have to be on our way tomorrow night while everyone in the big house is drinking wine and eating Christmas dinner. This rain is a blessing and a curse. It'll make it hard for the hounds to track us, but it'll slow us down, too."

Harriet and her brothers continued to talk in low tones until three other slaves, John, Peter, and Jane, joined them in the musty fodder shed. Ben and Robert had invited the three to join them as "Moses" led them all north.

"What about Ben and Old Rit?" Robert asked. "Old Rit is gonna sorely miss us. But we was about to be sold south anyway..." his voice drifted off.

"I think we can let Ben know we's here, 'cause we are gonna need some food," Harriet said. "Let's send John and Peter to talk to him in private. That way Old Rit won't find out we're here."

Everyone agreed and watched through the gaps in the wall of the fodder shed as John and Peter stepped outside, walked around to the cabin, and tapped on the door. Ben answered it, and soon he shut the door behind him and stood on the step talking to the two men. The conversation was short, and then Ben nodded and went back inside the cabin.

John and Peter hurried back to the fodder shed. "He was done surprised to hear Moses was here," Peter reported back. "But he was mighty glad to learn that the boys wouldn't be sold south after all. He said telling your ma would be a bad idea, but he's gonna slip some food to us when it gets dark."

True to his word, Harriet's father arrived with a stack of corncakes and hot tea. "Can't come in and see you," he whispered from the door. "But, Harriet, is that really you in there?"

"Yes, it's me," Harriet said, creeping to the door and reaching out for her father's hand. Ben squeezed Harriet's hand tightly.

"Lord knows I'd like to set eyes on you, child," Ben said. "But the fact is, soon as the boys are missed, Dr. Thompson's gonna ask me if I've seen them, or you, for that matter, and I gotta be able to say, 'No, sir, I ain't seen any of them since before Christmas. I ain't seen hide nor hair of them.'"

"I understand, Ben," Harriet replied softly, and she did. Her father had a reputation for always telling the truth, even to white people, and he wasn't about to have a lie on his conscience.

The following day, Christmas Day, was very difficult for Harriet. Her father sneaked by several times for a short talk, but she ached to be able to talk to her mother. She also began to worry that perhaps Henry had not gotten her message and would not be able to join them by the time they had to set out after nightfall. She also realized that Dr. Thompson would suspect that she had come back for her brothers when they were reported missing and would lead an intensive search for them all.

Thankfully, Henry showed up just before dark. Delighted that he had finally made it, Harriet hugged him tightly. Night fell, and it was soon time for them to move out. There were eight of them now, six men and two women, several other slaves having decided during the day to join the group for the journey north.

It was still raining heavily as the group left the fodder shed. When Harriet and her brothers passed their parents' cabin, she could not resist a peek in the window. She saw her mother sitting by the fire, rocking backward and forward. Harriet whispered, "God bless you, Old Rit," to herself and led her brothers away.

The group came to a sprawling oak tree, where Harriet's father was waiting for them. Ben was wearing a blindfold so as not to physically see Harriet and her brothers. Harriet tucked his hand under her arm, and Henry took his other arm. The three of them led the way down the dirt track that led into the woods.

"How you gonna know which way to go without the North Star to guide you?" her father asked.

"I know the way well now," Harriet replied quietly, "and the Lord, He goes before us and keeps us safe."

"I'll be prayin' that He does," Ben replied. "Now, you'd better leave me. I'm slowing you down."

Harriet gave her father one last hug and walked into the darkness. She led the group on, encouraging them to believe they could make it and guiding them to stations along the way and out of reach of hounds. They traveled, mainly on foot, through Dover, Smyrna, Canterbury, Camden, and St. George until they came to the home of Thomas Garrett in Wilmington. As usual, this kind, old Quaker welcomed Harriet and her band of runaway slaves and shared his family's food with them. He also provided new shoes for Harriet and a pair for one of the runaways who had lost his in a swamp.

Harriet was grateful for all Thomas did for them, especially since she knew how much he had sacrificed to help her and hundreds of other runaway slaves. William Still had read a newspaper article to Harriet that told how Thomas had been tried and found guilty of breaking the hated Fugitive Slave Act. Thomas's fine had been set so high that he lost everything he owned. But with the help of other abolitionists who came to his aid, he carried on his work with the Underground Railroad. His willingness to lose everything to help others gain freedom touched Harriet, as did his speech at his sentencing. She could still remember his exact reply as reported in the article William had read to her. The judge had declared the sentence and then turned to Thomas and said, "Garrett, let this be a lesson to you not to interfere hereafter with the cause of justice by helping runaway Negroes." Thomas had replied, "Judge, thee hasn't left me a dollar, but I wish to say to thee, and to all in this courtroom, that if anyone knows of a fugitive who wants shelter and a friend, send him to Thomas Garrett and he will befriend him!"

Indeed, Harriet was proud to introduce her three brothers to Thomas. They stayed two nights in his house before moving on.

Finally, on January 3, Harriet led the group across the Niagara Falls bridge into Canada. There were now more members of her family living in freedom than were still enslaved. But Harriet was not satisfied. For every slave she conducted north, she knew of hundreds who had been left behind. No sooner had she settled her brothers into their new life in Canada than she felt the urge to go south again.

Chapter 10

One More Soul Got Safe

Harriet pulled her coat tightly around her as she stepped into the small shed beside the church. It was a cold, windy morning in November 1856, and once again she found herself deep in "enemy" territory. She was waiting at this spot for four "parcels" to arrive—three men and a woman. She had not been told much about them except that they were all young, hardworking slaves, the type masters would look long and hard for and offer big rewards for. The very thought of this nauseated Harriet. As many times as she had come south, she could not adjust to the idea of one human being having the lawful right to own another.

Slowly the hubbub of slaves making their way into church filled the small shed. Some slaves laughed while others talked quietly together. Soon the service got under way, and Harriet hummed quietly to herself as the congregation sang a hymn. When the hymn was over, she was delighted to discover that if she put her ear to the wall of the shed, she could hear most of the words the preacher said. She knew from the man's voice and diction that he was white, but she listened carefully as he read a passage from the Bible. Then she heard him say, "Now we will recite the catechism. O Lord, attend unto our words."

"Amen," came the reply from the black slave congregation.

The catechism then began in earnest, with the preacher asking a question and the congregation answering in unison.

"Who gave you a master and a mistress?" the preacher intoned.

"God gave them to me," the congregation replied.

"Who says you must obey them?"

"God says that I must."

"What book tells you these things?"

"The Bible."

"How does God do all His work?"

"He always does it right."

"Does God love to work?"

"Yes, God is always at work."

Harriet had heard many catechisms before, but this was a new one, and listening to it made her anger burn. She did not want to hear any more of it, but the rhythm of the language drew her back.

"What does God say about your work?" the preacher continued in his question-and-answer style.

"He says that those who will not work shall not eat," the congregation replied.

"Did Adam and Eve have to work?"

"Yes, they had to keep the garden."

"Was it hard to keep that garden?"

"No, it was very easy."

"What makes the crops so hard to grow now?"

"Sin makes it hard."

"What makes you lazy?"

"My wicked heart."

"Who teaches you wicked things?"

"The devil."

Must you let the devil teach you?"

"No, I must not."

"Let the people say Amen."

"Amen," the congregation said exuberantly.

Another hymn began, but halfway through it Harriet fell into one of her sleeping spells. When she awoke, the wintry sun was low in the sky and four people sat huddled beside her. "Oh!" she exclaimed. "You must be the passengers."

"Yes, we are, and we sure hope you are Moses," one of them said.

Harriet nodded. "How long have you been here?"

"'Bout an hour or so. They told us you fall asleep sometimes, so we just be sitting here waiting for you to wake up," the only woman in the group replied. "My name's Eliza Nokey."

"And I'm Josiah Bailey, though everyone calls me Joe, and this here's my brother Bill, and my friend Peter Pennington."

Harriet smiled at them as she looked for signs as to what kind of passengers they would make. Would they be easily scared, or would they fearlessly follow her direction if things went wrong? She liked Joe instantly, but she knew his height could be a problem. Even though he was sitting down, she could see that he was tall and muscular and bald and had a telltale scar running under his right eye. These were all traits that were easy to broadcast and identify from a picture or written description. The others did not seem to have any particular markings that would make them easy to identify.

"We'll wait till dark before we leave," Harriet said. "What makes you ready to run now? Were you going to be sold south?"

Joe cleared his throat and replied in a low, musical voice. "I was sold, but not sold south. In fall, just after harvest, Mr. Hughlett, the man who'd been hirin' me for seven years, finally bought me from my master. Two thousand dollars he paid for me. I didn't see how it would make any difference to me if I was owned by Mr. Hughlett or hired by him. Either way I knows I'd do my best to work hard and keep outta trouble. But I was mistaken."

Harriet's heart sank when she heard the high price Joe had fetched. Hounds for miles around would surely join in the search for a piece of stolen property worth that much. Still she listened as Joe went on.

"The mornin' after I was purchased, my new owner came ridin' down to the slave quarters on his huge chestnut mare. He stopped outside my cabin and called for me. I thought he had some work for me, so I hurried out. 'What you want, master?' I asked. He said, 'Get down off that stoop and strip and take a lickin'.'"

Joe's eyes grew wide. "It was then I saw the rawhide whip in his hand. So I said to him, 'What's this about, master? Haven't I been faithful to you this last seven years? Haven't I worked through the sun and rain, early in the morning and late at night? Haven't I worked so well you could leave me without an overseer? What is your complaint against me?' Then I saw Master Hughlett smile at me. 'No, Joe,' he told me. 'I have no complaint against you. You're a good slave, and you've always worked well. But up until now I've hired you, and now I've bought you. You belong to me. You're my slave, and the first lesson all my slaves have to learn is that I'm master and they are never to resist anything I order them to do.' He cracked his whip. 'And I always begin by ordering my slaves to take a good lickin'. Now strip off and take it!' That's what he said to me, word for word. I'll never forget it as long as I live."

"What did you do?" Harriet asked, although she had already guessed the answer.

"Only thing I could do," Joe replied. "I stripped off and took the licking, but when it was over, I made a vow: That's the first and the last whippin' the master's ever gonna give me. And I spread the word that the next time someone heard from Moses, tell her she got herself a passenger."

The five of them kept talking in low voices until it was dark, and then Harriet said a prayer and led them out of the shed and on their way north.

It took every bit of Harriet's cunning to keep them safe. During the day they often hid in the holes where potatoes and other root vegetables were stored. Hounds and slave hunters often came within a few feet of their hiding places. Harriet borrowed various disguises for them, and they traveled by boat, by wagon, and on foot. At one stage Harriet decided it was too dangerous for them to all travel together, so she arranged for others to guide them separately to the home of her friend Sam Green. Sam was a free black man who lived in Dorchester County, Maryland. He was glad to help them, though he was aware of what expensive passengers he was harboring. He read Harriet and the others the words from a poster he had taken from a tree in town:

> HEAVY REWARD
> TWO THOUSAND SIX HUNDRED DOLLARS
> REWARD
>
> Ran away from the subscriber, on Saturday night, November 15th, 1856, Josiah and William Bailey and Peter Pennington. Joe is about 5 feet 10 inches in height, of a chestnut color, bald head, with a remarkable scar on one of his cheeks, not positive on which it is, but think it is on the left, under the eye, has intelligent countenance,

> active and well-made. His is about 28 years old. Bill is of a darker color, about 5 feet 8 inches in height, stammers a little when confused, well-made, and older than Joe, well dressed...Peter is smaller than either of the others, about 25 years of age, dark chestnut color, 5 feet 7 or 8 inches high.
>
> A reward of fifteen hundred dollars will be given to any person who will apprehend the said Joe Bailey and lodge him safely in the jail of Easton, Talbot Co., Md., and $300 for Bill and $800 for Peter."
>
> Signed, W.R. Hughlett
John C. Henry
T. Wright

"And that's not all," Sam continued. "I've seen a poster offering an even bigger reward for you, Harriet."

"How much was it?" she asked reluctantly.

"Twelve thousand dollars!" Sam replied. "Those slave owners are desperate to get their hands on Moses. It's not just the passengers you spirit away. It's all the others who get emboldened just hearing the stories about you and take off on their own. In some areas of Dorchester County, it's near impossible to keep a slave without chaining him up night and day."

Harriet laughed when she heard this. "That's just the way slave owners should feel, Sam!" she exclaimed. "I ain't gonna give up this work till every last slave is free."

"I know," Sam replied, "but I have a notion it's going to get a lot worse soon. Those slave owners are gettin' desperate."

Harriet had to agree with him. In the past year she had noticed more bounty hunters on the roads than ever before.

"You be extra careful now," Sam told her.

Sam Green's words were still echoing in her mind when Harriet reached the outskirts of Wilmington, Delaware, where the group had to cross the long bridge that led into the city. Getting across this bridge was a challenge for any runaway slave, but more so this time because of the high reward offered for the capture of those in the group. As a result the bridge was under constant surveillance by armed police. Harriet sent word to her old friend Thomas Garrett that she needed help getting across the bridge.

Thomas went right to work on the problem. He hired two wagonloads of bricklayers, who early in the morning set out across the bridge from Wilmington. This was a common occurrence, as slaves and other workers went out into the countryside during the day to work and returned to the city after dark. The police officers watching the bridge barely looked up as the two wagons filled with noisy bricklayers crossed over. And again they barely looked up when the wagons crossed the bridge back into the city in the early evening. In the bottom of the wagons on the way back into the city lay Harriet and the runaways she was conducting to freedom.

In Wilmington Thomas sheltered and fed them before they set out again. Four days later Harriet led the group into the Anti-Slavery Society's office in New York. Her friend Oliver Johnson, director of this branch of the society, was there to greet them warmly. He clapped Joe on the back. "Ha!" he said. "You must be Josiah Bailey. I'm glad to meet the man whose head is worth fifteen hundred dollars!"

"How'd you know my name?" Joe asked.

Oliver laughed. "We have a wanted poster for you right here in our office. The description is so close that no one could mistake you!"

Harriet watched as Joe's face fell. "Oh," Joe said. "And how far off is Canada?"

Oliver took Joe over to a large map of New York state that was pinned to the wall. "This is the way you will go from now on," he said, pointing to the railway line on the map. "It's three hundred miles up these tracks to Niagara, and when you cross the river there, you'll be free!"

"How am I gonna make it that far if everyone in New York knows me?" Joe asked.

Harriet hooked her arm in his. "Joe, you've trusted the Lord six times so far, and He ain't let you down yet. He won't let you down on the seventh, no, sir, He won't."

Both Harriet and Oliver continued to encourage Joe to have hope that he would make it safely to freedom, but a gloom settled over him. He became convinced that someone would recognize him and he would be arrested before he ever reached Canada. For the rest of the trip, Joe never said a word. He spent his time looking nervously around him or with his face buried in his hands.

Despite Joe's behavior, Harriet guided the group of runaway slaves through New York state and right up to Niagara Falls. The train rumbled onto the suspension bridge that straddled the falls linking the United States and Canada.

"Joe, come over here and look at these mighty falls," Harriet said.

Joe sat motionless, his head buried in his hands while the others peered down at Niagara Falls from the window of the railway carriage.

Finally Harriet felt the carriage roll over the slight peak of the bridge and gently slope toward Canada. Harriet knew that the peak of the bridge marked the boundary between Canada and the United States. She walked over to Joe and shook him so hard he nearly fell off his seat. "Joe! You just shook the lion's paw." It was her way of saying they were now in Canada, but her meaning was lost on Joe, who looked at her with glassy eyes. "You're in Canada now, Joe. You're a free man!"

This time Joe understood her meaning. He leaped out of his seat and raised his hands high. Tears began to stream down his face, and he began to sing.

Glory to God and Jesus too,
One more soul got safe.
Oh, go and carry the news,
One more soul got safe.

He sang the song over and over as the train rumbled off the bridge and made its way the short distance to St. Catharines.

By now Joe's excitement had touched many of those riding in the carriage. Tears were streaming down the faces of men and women alike. One white woman handed Joe her finely embroidered handkerchief for him to wipe his tears away.

Tears flooded Harriet's eyes, too. All of the effort, all of the money, all of the danger she put herself in were made worthwhile by Joe's exuberant celebration of his freedom. To a person who had been owned by another all his life, this was the sweetest moment of all in the world. One more soul had "got safe," but there were still many more souls who were not free, locked in slavery in the South. Among them were Harriet's own parents, Ben and Old Rit. As the train approached the station in St. Catharines, Harriet promised herself that she would not rest until every enslaved soul in the United States was finally free and able to experience for himself or herself the moment Joe and the other three runaway slaves were caught up in.

Chapter 11

Free at Last

Harriet awoke with her heart pounding and her body shaking violently. She had just had a bad dream—a terrible dream where her father was stripped to the waist and being whipped by a group of leering white men while her mother stood beside him and screamed for Harriet to help them. Harriet knew she would not get back to sleep, so she got up and lit the fire in the stove to make a pot of coffee.

Two hours later Harriet arrived at her job as a maid in a hotel in Cape May, New Jersey. But as she scrubbed floors and made beds, her thoughts were never far from Ben and Old Rit. Somewhere deep inside she was sure her parents were in trouble and needed her help. By the end of the day Harriet knew that she could not rest until she had rescued them both. Harriet had just one problem: Any rescue attempt would take a lot of money. There was no way two old people could walk most of the thousand miles from Maryland to Canada, if indeed they were in good enough health to walk at all. For such a trip Harriet would have to pay for other means of transport. And that was the problem; she had little money at that moment. She had given most of her money to a family of runaway slaves who were trying to set up a small farm back in St. Catharines. Yet she felt she needed to do something, and do it now.

Harriet decided to appeal to her friends in the Anti-Slavery Society in New York for the needed money. On June 12, 1857, she used what little money she had to buy a train ticket to New York City. As she stepped onto the train, she made a promise to herself: *I'm not going to eat or drink until I get money to take me down after the old people.*

With that settled in her mind, Harriet sat watching the scenery flash before her. From time to time she took out a book she always carried with her and scanned a few pages. She could not read a word of the book, of course, but she had made a little mark on the front of it so that she would know which way to hold it. Since her wanted posters all pointed out that Harriet could not read, she decided that pretending to read would throw any potential slave hunter off track.

By midmorning Harriet had reached New York City, and she went straight to the Anti-Slavery Society office. Inside the office a new secretary sat behind the front desk. When she saw Harriet her eyes grew wide as she spoke.

"So you are *the* Harriet Tubman, the one they call Moses," the woman said. "Why, just this morning we received a newspaper article about you. Here, listen to what it says." She reached over and picked up a newspaper clipping from her desk. "'It is now come to pass that rewards are offered for the apprehension of the Negro woman who is denuding the fields of their laborers and cabins of their human livestock. She is a plain woman, short of stature, upper front teeth missing, with a habit of abruptly falling asleep. She looks harmless, but she carries a pistol. Various rewards for her capture totaled $40,000 to the man bringing her in dead or alive.'"

Harriet laughed. "I am worth a lot more than that to the good Lord!"

"Harriet, how good to see you," came a voice from behind her. She swung around to see Oliver Johnson standing there. "Come into my office," Oliver said. "We need to talk. Things have taken a serious turn for the worse, as I'm sure you're well aware."

Harriet and Oliver talked for over an hour about how conditions had grown worse since Harriet's last trip south. Her friend Sam Green, the free black man who had often helped her, had been convicted and sent to jail for ten years simply for possessing a copy of the book *Uncle Tom's Cabin*, which had been banned in the South. While this was a severe penalty, it was in keeping with the current ugly mood of Southern slave owners. New laws restricting black people, both slave and free, were being written every week. And it was all because of a court case involving a slave named Dred Scott. Twenty years before, Dred Scott's master had taken him on a visit from the slave state of Missouri into the slave-free state of Illinois and territory of Wisconsin. When he got to Wisconsin, Dred Scott demanded that his master free him since he was now in a free territory. His master refused and took him south again. When Dred Scott got back to Missouri, he sought out an antislavery lawyer, with the intention of suing his master for his freedom.

The case became a rallying call to both pro- and antislavery groups, and after a lot of stalling, it finally made its way to the Supreme Court in 1856. The two questions the court considered were, did Dred Scott's residence in a free territory during the 1830s make him a free man, and as a slave now back in Missouri, did he have the right to sue in a federal court?

The Supreme Court's ruling in the case had been handed down two months before—two days after the inauguration of newly elected President James Buchanan. The decision had divided the United States as never before. The court had decided that a slave could never sue for his freedom. But the justices went much further in their ruling. They declared that no black person—slave or free—or anyone with black ancestry could become a citizen of the United States. The Supreme

Court also declared that Congress could not prohibit slavery in a territory, thus making all of Congress's laws against slavery in new territories illegal.

While Southern slave owners rejoiced over the Dred Scott decision, many towns and cities in the North announced that they would not accept the Supreme Court's ruling.

"The battle lines are being drawn. The stranglehold the South has on our people must be broken," Oliver concluded.

"Amen!" Harriet replied. "Our people must go free. They must!"

"Anyway, what brings you to New York?" Oliver finally asked.

"I feel my parents are in danger, and I must rescue them," she replied, "and I came to ask you for twenty dollars to do it."

"Twenty dollars? That's a lot of money, Harriet. I'm afraid we don't have that much right now."

Harriet thought for a moment, then spoke very deliberately. "I've come here for money to rescue my parents, and I'm not going to leave here or eat or drink until I get it."

"Whatever you say," Oliver sighed. "You know I would give it to you if I had it."

"I know," Harriet replied. "Don't you worry yourself. God will provide it for me."

Harriet left Oliver's office and settled herself into a chair by the front desk. She tucked a knitted shawl around herself and settled in for a long wait. Within minutes she had fallen into one of her deep sleeps. She awoke around dinnertime, and it took her a moment or two to recall where she was. Then she saw something poking out of her shawl—it was a ten-dollar bill! Harriet unwrapped her shawl, and dollar notes fell out all around her. "What's this?" she asked the secretary.

The secretary grinned at Harriet. "It's been the strangest thing, Miss Harriet. Men and women have been coming in here all afternoon bringing bits of money for you. Word must have gotten around that you needed some. I don't even know who half of the people were."

Harriet smiled back. "God—He's helped me six times, and He never failed me on the seventh either!" she said, repeating a phrase she had often used. When she had counted the money, she had sixty dollars. Harriet immediately headed to the South to rescue her parents.

When she reached Bucktown, Maryland, thirty-six-year-old Harriet began to walk in a stooped-over position and assume the mannerisms of an old woman. She also bought two chickens, tied their legs together and hung them over her shoulder. In this way she hoped that people, some of whom knew her, would just think she was an old woman taking chickens to the market and would pay her no mind.

Harriet began to make her way along the road that led from Bucktown past the old plantation where her parents still lived. As she walked along she became aware of the clap of horse's hooves approaching from behind. Her first reaction was to run and hide in the bushes at the side of the road, but they were mostly brambles and thorns, and Harriet did not want to tear her clothes or her skin on them. So she kept her eyes straight ahead and continued to walk in her stooped position. The sound of the horse's hooves grew louder. Harriet moved as far to the side of the road as she could as the horse drew alongside her. She tried to keep her fears under control, but this was not easy to do when she looked up at the rider of the horse and into the face of Dr. Thompson.

Dr. Thompson drew on his cigar and took a long look at Harriet from under his sweat-stained Panama hat. Harriet knew she must act fast before her old master recognized her. In one swift motion she reached up and quickly pulled undone the knot binding the two chickens together. The birds squawked as they tumbled to the ground. In a cloud of dust and feathers they fluttered down the road away from Harriet, who turned and began to chase them.

Dr. Thompson thought it was a great joke. He turned and watched Harriet run after the chickens in her stooped-over pose. "Go on, Granny!" he called after her. "I'll bet on the chickens, though." He let out a raucous laugh.

Harriet continued to chase the chickens until she heard her old master gallop off on his horse. She let out a deep sigh of relief, though she was careful to keep her stooped-over pose. She continued on down the road in the direction of the plantation. As she walked, the late afternoon sun began to drop behind the horizon, and darkness crept across the countryside. When it was dark, Harriet abandoned her stooped posture and began to make her way in and out of the shadows. Finally she reached the slave quarters of the old plantation. Quickly and quietly she made her way to her parents' cabin and knocked on the door.

Old Rit opened the door slightly and peered into the darkness. "Who is it?" she asked.

"It's Harriet!"

Harriet waited anxiously to see how her mother would respond. Would she let out one of her loud emotional outbursts at the news and alert the whole plantation to Harriet's presence, or would she keep her emotions in check until long after they had left the plantation behind? To Harriet's relief, Old Rit kept her emotions in check. "Is that really you, Harriet?" was all she said as she swung the door wide open.

Inside the tiny cabin, Harriet stared into the eyes of her mother for the first time in eight years.

"I didn't think I'd ever see you again," Old Rit said as the two women embraced. Harriet's shoulder was soon wet with Old Rit's tears.

Ben quickly left his perch by the fireplace and engulfed Harriet in a big hug.

"I've come to take you away," Harriet said.

"Not a moment too soon," Old Rit replied. "On Monday they gonna try your pappy for helping a runaway escape."

"So that was it!" Harriet exclaimed. "I knew something was terribly wrong."

"I didn't do what they claim," Ben said, "but what does that matter? I'm an old slave. Ain't nobody gonna believe me. Besides, if I get thrown in jail, the master don't need to feed and house me no more."

Harriet hugged her father again. "Ain't nobody gonna try you here, Ben. We movin' your trial to a higher court—the court of freedom in Canada."

It was obvious to Harriet that her parents could not walk even part of the way to freedom, so she began to search for a plan. After talking to her father for several minutes, things began to formulate in her head.

Harriet left her parents at the cabin and made her way to the far meadow of the plantation, where an old mare had been put out to pasture. She captured the animal and led it to the back of the barn, where she quietly hitched it to a rickety old wagon. An hour and a half after leaving her parents' cabin, she returned to it. Quickly she bundled her parents into the wagon, and they were off.

They rode all night in the wagon, and as the sun began to rise, they pulled into the dense woods at the side of the road and hid. Ben and Old Rit slept while Harriet kept watch. Once darkness had descended, they again set out. After three nights of travel, they arrived at Thomas Garrett's house in Wilmington, Delaware. Thomas fed and sheltered Harriet and her parents for two nights before they set out on the next leg of their journey, through Philadelphia and New York City and finally by train into Canada. It was a wonderful moment for Harriet and her brothers and sister when Ben and Old Rit stepped off the train in St. Catharines—free at last.

Everyone back at the old plantation in Maryland knew at once that only "Moses" could have led two elderly people north, and news of Harriet's bold feat quickly spread throughout the South. Proslavery campaigners labeled the rescue of her parents as "cruel an act as was ever performed by a child towards parents." One politician named John Bell Robinson, in his new book on the benefits of slavery, openly criticized Harriet for rescuing Ben and Old Rit:

> The most noted point in the act of horror was the bringing away from ease and comfortable homes two old slaves over seventy years of age [Harriet's parents]. Now there are no old people of any color more caressed and better taken care of than the old worn-out slaves of the South, except for the wealthy whites, who are few in number.... Those old slaves had earned their living while young, and a home for themselves when past labor, and had sat down at ease around the plentiful board of their master, whose duty it was to support them through old age, and see them well taken care of in sickness, and when dead to give them a respectable burying. This ignorant woman [Harriet] must have been persuaded

> and bewildered by flattery by some fiendish source, or she certainly would not have been guilty of such a diabolical act of wickedness and cruelty to her parents.

Harriet already had a reply to this criticism. It was printed in a book called *The Refugee: or Narratives of Fugitive Slaves* by Benjamin Drew. Drew had interviewed Harriet about her experience of slavery and recorded her statements. Among the recorded statements in the book, Harriet had said:

> I grew up like a neglected weed—ignorant of liberty, having no experience of it. I was not happy or contented: every time I saw a white man I was afraid of being carried away. I had two sisters carried away in a chain gang—one of them left two children. We were always uneasy. Now I've been free, I know what slavery is. I have seen hundreds of escaped slaves but I never saw one who was willing to go back and be a slave.... I think slavery is the next thing to hell.

As 1857 drew to a close, Harriet made a home for her parents and watched for the gathering clouds of war. She was certain that Southern slave owners were not going to give up their "property" without a fight. She was just as certain that the time was very near when slaves would rise up with one voice to claim their freedom.

Chapter 12

The Battle of Troy

The winter of 1857 proved to be unusually harsh, and Harriet's aged parents found it difficult to adjust to the three-foot snowdrifts that often kept them stuck inside the house for weeks at a time. By Christmas Harriet realized that Ben and Old Rit would be better off in a warmer climate. But where? Finally she settled on the small town of Auburn, New York. She had passed through this town many times. It was a stop on the Underground Railroad, and many Quakers and abolitionists were living there.

Harriet knew it was risky settling her parents in the United States, but she felt that her family would have many powerful friends to help them if they got into trouble with slave hunters. The United States senator for New York, William Seward, had become an admirer of Harriet, and he offered to sell her a house and piece of property he owned on South Street in Auburn at a very reasonable rate of interest. This was a brave act on Senator Seward's part because he planned to run for president in the next election, and if word got out that he had sold land to a fugitive slave, he would be knocked out of the race. He might even be tried for making an illegal land sale.

Early in 1858 Harriet moved her few belongings into the house on South Street and made a home for her parents. Someone gave her mother a rocking chair, and Old Rit spent many happy hours talking, singing, and praying with Harriet's many visitors. Harriet's father tried to help with work around the place as much as he could, but he was too old to do much more than split kindling wood or weed the garden. Still, they were all happy together.

The battle over slavery continued to be fought in words, with each side holding its own conferences. In August 1858 some of the slave states held the Eastern Shore Convention, where Southern lawyers dredged up old proslavery laws and reinstated them. One of their acts, which particularly chilled Harriet's blood, was the reapplying of an 1825 law that called for free blacks in Maryland to be either removed from the state or made into slaves again. Much to the abolitionists' horror, eighty-nine free blacks in Maryland were rounded up and sold to white owners.

Meanwhile abolitionists were holding their own conventions and rallies. One white man who appeared at some of these meetings was John Brown, who had a daring plan to free slaves. At nearly sixty years of age, he had given up on waiting for peaceful methods of protest to free the slaves. Instead, he wanted to build an army of free blacks and white men in Canada and the United States and fight slaveholders in the Appalachian states, leading the slaves to freedom in Canada or the Northwest. For his plan to work he needed the trust and support of top black abolitionists.

Harriet had followed John Brown's plans from a distance, but she was surprised when he arrived on the doorstep to see her. She was staying in St. Catharines at the time and knew that John Brown must have gone to some trouble to track her down. At this meeting John Brown outlined his plan to Harriet. She was enthusiastic about it and promised she would encourage free black men in Canada and the United States to join in the plan when the time was right.

John Brown's visit and Harriet's support of him thrust her into the national spotlight as never before. She was asked to describe her experiences and give her opinions at many large gatherings. At first this was difficult for Harriet, who felt nervous speaking to large groups of white people. Soon Harriet discovered that allowing the audience to ask her questions was the easiest way for her to present the needs and perspective of the slaves and fugitives.

Harriet always used everyday examples to get her point across. Many Americans thought that the best solution to the slave problem was to ship all black people back to Africa. In fact the idea was not new. In 1822 President James Monroe and many other prominent and rich white men had come up with the idea of starting a colony for returned slaves in Africa. They set up the American Colonization Society and began shipping free blacks and slaves "home" to the newly founded country of Liberia. Harriet, however, did not agree with this solution to the slave problem. When she was questioned about it, she always told her audience a story about onions and garlic.

"There was once a man who sowed onions and garlic for his cows to eat, but he found that the milk and butter had a very strong taste," she would say. "So he decided to sow clover instead, but he soon found that the wind had blown the onion and garlic seeds all over his clover field and they grew alongside the clover. And so it is with America. The white people brought the black people over to work in drudgery, and now that the 'taste' of them has become unpleasant, they are trying to root them out and ship them back to Africa. But," she concluded, "they can't do it. We're rooted here, and they cannot pull us up."

Harriet continued to speak at various engagements and go south on difficult "missions." Many antislavery groups tried to stop her from going south at all, fearing she would be captured and burned at the stake as a warning to other blacks. But Harriet was not worried about such an outcome. She told everyone that she would live until the day the Lord chose to take her home.

In September 1859, though, Harriet reached the exhaustion point. The years of poor diet, constant stress, caring for her parents, and continually working for the abolitionist cause finally caught up with her. She found herself flat on her back in New Bedford, Massachusetts, unable to carry on her work. Her illness probably saved her life because at the same time, John Brown and his two sons were planning a raid on the U.S. arsenal at Harpers Ferry, Virginia. Harriet, whom John Brown referred to as General Tubman, wanted desperately to be with him, but she was not well enough to travel.

On the morning of October 17, 1859, Harriet awoke with a foreboding feeling. "I know something has gone terribly wrong," she told the woman looking after her.

"Wrong with what?" the woman asked.

"With Captain Brown," Harriet said, suddenly feeling cold. "Something terrible has happened to him."

Later that day Harriet heard the news that the U.S. arsenal at Harpers Ferry had been seized and John Brown and twenty-one of his followers were holding sixty local men hostage there.

Harriet groaned when she heard the news. She had a feeling things had gone wrong with the plan. And they had. The next day's newspaper bore the news that Colonel Robert E. Lee and his federal troops had routed John Brown's men, killing ten of them, including three black men and both of John Brown's sons. John Brown himself had been captured, and a date was already set for his treason trial. Harriet was devastated when the newspaper article was read aloud to her. She had such high hopes for John Brown and his men. Still, she admired the way he continued to denounce slavery right up to the time he was hanged six weeks later.

Like many black people throughout North America, Harriet never forgot John Brown's last words. On the gallows Brown said, "Now, if it is deemed necessary that I should forfeit my life for the furtherance of the ends of justice, and mingle my blood further with the blood of my children, and with the blood of millions in this slave country, whose rights are disregarded by wicked, cruel, and unjust enactments—I say let it be done."

After John Brown's death, white people in the South became even more convinced that some great plan was afoot to liberate their slaves. Harriet wished there were, but instead the abolitionist movement plodded on, holding meetings and spiriting small bands of slaves away from their plantations whenever they could. Harriet continued to play her part in the process, mainly through inspiring others and carrying the message of just how horrible it was to be owned by another human being.

On April 27, 1860, as Harriet made her way by train to Boston to speak at the New England Anti-Slavery Society conference, she stopped off in Troy, New York, to visit a relative living there. No sooner had she stepped off the train than she heard about the plight of Charles Nalle, a runaway slave from Virginia.

Trying to make his way to Canada, Nalle had been captured near Troy, and his fate was about to be decided in court before a federal commissioner. It seemed inevitable that he would be ordered returned to his owner in Virginia. However, many of the residents of Troy were opposed to slavery—and particularly to the Fugitive Slave Act. A number of them had gathered outside the courthouse at the corner of State and First Streets. Proslavery supporters had also gathered, and an ugly mood had settled over the crowd.

When Harriet heard about what was happening, she made her way straight to the courthouse to see what could be done to help Nalle. As soon as she arrived, she began to think like a general. She surveyed the thousand or so people who were crowded around the courthouse. The crowd was not big enough! If she was going to rescue Nalle, it would take more people than that to create enough chaos to snatch him away.

Hardly stopping to think through what she was doing, Harriet motioned to several boys, who gathered around her. "Go through town yelling 'Fire! Fire!'" she told them.

Harriet knew that more people would pour out into the streets when the fire bells were rung and the fire wagons came barreling down the street. Sure enough, the plan worked, and soon the crowd swelled to five thousand people, both blacks and whites.

In the meantime Harriet, stooped-over and pretending to be an old woman, pushed her way to the second-floor courtroom to view the proceedings for herself. The courtroom was packed, and she was forced to stand at the back. It wasn't long before the federal commissioner rendered his decision in the case. As expected, Nalle was to be returned that evening to his owner in Virginia. However, Nalle's lawyer immediately sought permission to appeal the decision and, upon such permission being granted, left the court to arrange an appeal hearing.

As everyone else waited in the courtroom, a voice from the street below began to call up at them. "We'll buy his freedom. What price does his master want for him?" the voice asked.

The owner's representative, who was present in the courtroom, went to the window and called, "Twelve hundred dollars."

People in the crowd began to pledge money for the purchase price, and soon they had twelve hundred dollars. "We have raised the money," they called back.

Harriet watched the surprised look on the representative's face. The man went to the window, but instead of accepting the money, he raised the price. "Fifteen hundred dollars," he called down.

The crowd was infuriated by the representative's actions and began to hurl curses and abuse at him. "I'll pay two hundred dollars for his rescue but not one cent to his master," someone in the crowd yelled.

A loud cheer went up from the crowd, and many of those in the courtroom joined in.

The lawyer soon returned to the court with an order from a judge that Nalle be moved to a courtroom farther down the street, where an appeal of the decision would be heard right away. Handcuffed, Nalle was led away.

Harriet quickly seized the moment. She raced to the courtroom window. "Here he comes. Take him!" she called to the crowd below.

The crowd surged forward. As the police tried to lead Nalle from the courthouse, Harriet bolted down the stairs. She pushed a policeman to the ground, grabbed hold of Nalle's arm, and would not let go. A police officer struck her across the head with his billy club, but still Harriet would not let go. She kept pulling on Nalle, trying to wrench him away from his escort's grasp. The crowd pressed in around them. Fists and other weapons began to fly, and gunshots were fired, but Harriet held firm.

Harriet was clubbed several more times, but she would not let go. When she and Nalle were both knocked to the ground, she quickly placed her sunbonnet on his head. When he was hauled back to his feet, it was hard for the police and the proslavery members in the crowd to spot him.

Blood began to flow in the streets of Troy. A pitched battle was now under way between police and proslavery advocates and the abolitionists. In the midst of the melee, Harriet determinedly kept trying to pull Nalle free. Finally the confused policemen let their charge go. Harriet quickly guided Nalle to the bank of the Hudson River, where he was bundled facedown into the bottom of a skiff, and a sympathetic ferryman rowed him across.

Harriet and four hundred others boarded a steam ferry that was about to cross to the other side of the river, where they hoped to see Nalle safely on his way to freedom in Canada. However, the federal commissioner had telegraphed ahead, and when Nalle reached the other side, he was arrested by a local constable and barricaded in the third-floor office of the local justice of the peace.

When Harriet and the others discovered what had happened, they stormed the office. Several men were shot as they tried to make their way up the stairs. Eventually, though, the group made it upstairs, where a huge black man battered open the office door. No sooner had he done this than a constable struck him over the head with a hatchet. The burly black man collapsed in the doorway, preventing those inside from closing the door. Harriet led the charge into the office. She and several other women leaped over the fallen man's body and overpowered the now frightened constables huddled inside.

Nalle was bundled downstairs, where a man offered the use of his horse and buggy when he heard what was happening. The badly beaten fugitive slave staggered into the buggy and was gone.

Battered and bruised, Harriet was sheltered by abolitionists in Troy, where she stayed hidden for several days, until her strength returned and the police stopped searching for her. She was relieved to hear that Charles Nalle had made it to

Schenectady, where abolitionists sheltered him and helped him on his way to freedom in Canada.

Eventually Harriet continued on her journey to Boston, the hero of what had already become known as the Battle of Troy.

Chapter 13

"This Is the First Day We Have Ever Had a Country"

The rescue of Charles Nalle brought even more fame to Harriet, who soon found herself the honored guest in many of the finest homes in the North. In Boston, newspaper owner Franklin Sanborn introduced her to Ralph Waldo Emerson, Amos Alcott and his daughter Louisa May, and Susan B. Anthony. They all became lifelong friends of Harriet.

In Boston, as in the rest of the United States, political issues were being hotly debated. It was an election year, and in a surprising upset, a little-known lawyer named Abraham Lincoln had won the Republican nomination for president over Harriet's friend Senator William Seward. The Northern Democrats' candidate was Stephen Douglas, and the debates between him and Lincoln were closely followed by millions of people. The main issue they argued had to do with states' rights: Did individual states have the right to make up their own minds about slavery, or was it the job of the federal government to set laws and force individual states to follow them? As far as the issue of slavery went, Lincoln believed that states in the South had a constitutional right to preserve slavery if they so wished but that Congress could make laws that would stop its expansion into new states or territories. Lincoln personally hated slavery, but as a lawyer he did not see how Congress could override individual states on the issue.

Harriet followed the election with great interest. She did not like Abraham Lincoln, because he did not promise to ban slavery in all of the United States if he was elected president, but she liked Stephen Douglas even less.

On Election Day, November 6, 1860, Lincoln beat Douglas by nearly 500,000 votes to become the sixteenth president of the United States.

Southern states did not trust Lincoln's promise that he would not interfere with states' rights. They were sure he was secretly working with abolitionists, and so in December, South Carolina seceded from the United States of America.

The battle over slavery had now moved from one of words to one of action, though not outright war. Harriet, though, remained firm in her belief that war was only a matter of time. "Others say peace, peace as much as they like," she told friends, "but I know there is going to be war."

While all this was going on, Harriet continued to do what she could for slaves. In November she made her last trip to Maryland to serve as a conductor for the Underground Railroad. Her assignment was to bring a slave named Stephen Ennets, his wife, Maria, and their three small children safely north. As with her previous trips, Harriet managed to guide them all to safety. Altogether she had made nineteen trips to the South, rescuing more than three hundred men, women, and children. She would smile as she told people, "On my Underground Railroad, I never run my train off the track and I never lost a passenger."

Harriet watched as other Southern states followed South Carolina's lead. By February 1, 1861, Mississippi, Florida, Alabama, Louisiana, and Georgia had all announced they too were leaving the Union. Representatives from these states held a conference the following week in Montgomery, Alabama, and declared to the world that they were now the Confederate States of America, complete with their own president—Jefferson Davis.

Now the United States was not united at all but was two countries, with two presidents and two sets of laws. However, many places in the South belonged to the federal government, and once Lincoln took office as president, he was determined to protect them. One of these places was Fort Sumter, a federal Army post located in Charleston Harbor, South Carolina. The Confederate South considered Fort Sumter to be theirs and on April 12, 1861, opened fire on the fort. Harriet was right—war had begun.

Harriet was visiting St. Catharines when the first shots of the Civil War were fired. She hurried south to see what she could do to help. For the next three months, she followed the Union army led by General Butler as it marched through Maryland on its way to defend Washington, D.C., from Confederate attack. She busied herself encouraging Maryland slaves to escape across the Union army lines and helped to take care of them when they did. As far as Harriet knew, she was the only woman in the United States working alongside the army, but she did not care. She could handle a musket as well as any man, and she knew the countryside like the back of her hand.

The black slaves who ran away were in a strange position as far as the law went. President Lincoln declared them contraband, not free men and women but no longer slaves either. This legal limbo meant that they could not be drafted into the Union army, a position that infuriated Harriet. The Union comprised twenty-three states, with a total population of twenty-two million people. The Confederates, on the other hand, had eleven states and nine million people, four million of whom were slaves. Harriet was sure that if Lincoln freed the slaves from the South and allowed them to fight as part of the Union army, the Union could win the war quickly. Otherwise, she predicted, the war would drag on for a very long time. To Harriet's dismay, Lincoln would not change the legal status of slaves.

"They may send the flower of their young men down south, to die of the fever in the summer and the ague in the winter," Harriet told her friend, famous journalist Lydia Child. "They may send them one year, two year, three year, till they tire of sending or till they use up the young men. All of no use. God is ahead of Mister Lincoln. God won't let Mister Lincoln beat the South till he does the right thing. Mister Lincoln, he is a great man, and I'm a poor Negro; but this Negro can tell Mister Lincoln how to save the money and the young men. He can do it by setting the Negroes free."

Harriet added another of her homey comparisons to her remarks. "Suppose there was an awfully big snake down there on the floor. He bites you. You send for the doctor to cut [treat] the bite; but the snake, he rolls up there, and while the doctor is doing it, he bites you again. The doctor cuts down that bite, but while he's doing it the snake springs up and bites you again, and so he keeps doing till you kill him. That's what Mister Lincoln ought to know."

The big snake, of course, was slavery, and Harriet was sure that the Civil War would never be won until slavery was defeated in the South once and for all.

Early in 1862 Harriet received word that Governor Andrew of Massachusetts wanted to see her. She hurried to visit him. The governor asked her to go south to work with the contraband. Large numbers of slaves were pouring into the Union camp at Port Royal, South Carolina, asking for protection and looking for ways to help the Union win the war. However, Governor Andrew told Harriet, there were problems. Southern blacks did not completely trust Northern white soldiers, and many misunderstandings arose because of the slaves' Southern accent and their use of strange combinations of African words. The Department of the South needed someone who could bridge the gap between white soldiers and the black contraband. Governor Andrew said he had asked many people who could best handle the problem, and one name kept coming up time after time—Moses! Since Harriet had been looking for some way to become more useful in the war, she agreed to go as soon as she found someone to take care of her parents.

In May Harriet found herself sailing out of New York Harbor aboard the transport ship USS *Atlantic.* Her destination was Beaufort County, South Carolina, where she was to report to General Hunter, commander of the Union forces there.

As the USS *Atlantic* steamed down the coast of North America past New Jersey and Chesapeake Bay, Harriet learned more about the challenges that lay ahead. The small county of Beaufort was on the southernmost coast of South Carolina, right next to Georgia and only a few miles from Savannah. It was made up of several islands and was crisscrossed with rivers that offered excellent shelter to ships. Until six months before, Port Royal, a town on St. Helena island, had been the site of an important harbor for the Confederacy. However, Union soldiers had overwhelmed the area and driven off the Confederate forces. Now Port

Royal was a vital coal-refueling port for the Union ships that were blockading the Confederate coastline.

When the Confederate army retreated from the area, plantation owners realized they were no longer protected, and so they took what they could and abandoned their plantations. They tried to force their slaves to flee inland with them, but many refused. The unlucky slaves were shot by their owners; the lucky ones escaped into the swamps and made their way through Union lines to safety.

Of course how "lucky" some of these escaped slaves were was a matter of opinion, as Harriet found out when she disembarked in Beaufort. Throngs of small, near-naked black children swarmed around her as she made her way to General Hunter's headquarters. Many of the children had open sores on their bodies, and their bellies bulged, a telltale sign of malnutrition. Young and old men sat around fishing while women stared listlessly into space. Harriet had never seen so much human need clustered into one place before.

Soon Harriet was in General Hunter's office. The general greeted her enthusiastically and then got straight to the point. "Harriet," he said, as he settled into his chair, "we have a very difficult situation here. The black people who have flooded in to seek our protection are hostages to this war we are fighting. Some of them are sick or wounded, and all of them are hungry and disoriented. I know that most of them have never been this far from their home plantations before, and they are scared.

What is more, they are not free and therefore cannot leave to make their own way in this world. But they are not slaves, either, and therefore have no slave owner to feed and clothe them and tell them what to do each day. Quite frankly, I have asked the government for the money to feed them all and teach them how to get gainful employment, but it has been denied me." He flung his arms in the air. "I do not know what to do with them all, but I do know that if something is not done, we will have many more deaths on our hands. That's why you are here, though we could no doubt do with a thousand Harriet Tubmans!"

Harriet sat quietly for a minute or so, then replied, "I will do my best, General, and I will pray that the good Lord guides my actions."

"Wonderful!" General Hunter responded. "I have a little house ready for you, which I think you will find adequate, and of course you can draw soldier's rations. Two hundred dollars has been set aside for your immediate use, and you will receive a soldier's pay, though...umm...owing to the peculiar nature of the arrangement, I can't promise you when that will happen."

Harriet nodded. She knew she was the only black woman employed by the Union army and realized that that posed some problems for the system. Still, she was eager to do what she could—she just had no idea how difficult it was going to be.

Instead of being welcomed by the former slaves, Harriet met with open hostility. By the end of the first week, she had hardly made a friend. "You keep your Yankee hands off my body," spat one old woman when Harriet offered to bath her infected foot. And a young boy told her, "My ma says you've got nothin' to say to us. You eat good every day, taking them rations like a white soldier."

So that's it! Harriet thought to herself. *Slaves this far south don't know about my work on the Underground Railroad. They must think I have always lived an easy life up north, and now here I am eating three meals a day and living like a white mistress!*

Harriet realized she would never win their hearts and minds until she learned to speak and live like them. She marched straight to the army quartermaster and informed him that she would no longer draw her rations. She would make her own way from now on.

That proved to be the key to winning the hearts and minds of South Carolina blacks. It was not easy. Each evening Harriet made pies, gingerbread, and root beer in her little house and then employed several of the black women to sell it to Union soldiers. The venture made enough money to feed Harriet and provide an income for four other families. Soon other contraband started hanging around Harriet's house asking what they could do to earn money.

Harriet took the two hundred dollars from the government and bought enough timber and other supplies to build a long shed. She then employed several of the black men to construct the building. Once the structure had been erected, Harriet set it up as a laundry, where the women could contract to do a soldier's laundry for him. Two months after Harriet's arrival, Beaufort was a hive of small industries and groups of people who helped one another.

During this time General Hunter told Harriet that he wanted to be ready as soon as President Lincoln gave the orders to allow contraband to become regular soldiers. And so the First South Carolina Regiment was started. It was entirely made up of former slaves, and although it was not an official regiment of the Union army, it drilled and practiced while waiting for the opportunity to fight the Confederacy.

Harriet often stopped to watch the First South Carolina Regiment drill as she made her way to the hospital. Tireless as ever, she had selected the hospital as her next "project." It was an enormous challenge. The hospital director, an abolitionist named Henry Durrant, was overwhelmed with the lack of supplies and nurses. Harriet did what she could. Each morning she hurried to the stately Southern mansion that had been converted into the hospital. Inside, all of the grand furniture had been stripped out, and rows of men, women, and children lay groaning on straw pallets. Many suffered from gunshot wounds, dysentery, malaria, smallpox, malnutrition, or a combination of these illnesses. The smell in the place was so overwhelming that Harriet had to steel herself to walk through the door.

Inside the hospital Harriet spent her days bathing flyblown wounds, soothing babies who were burning with fever, and turning women who were delirious from smallpox. She also searched the swamps and fields for plants and roots that looked similar to the ones Old Rit had used to cure diseases and mixed up concoctions of her own that soon became legendary.

Within months Harriet's skill with nursing was known all over the region. She found herself traveling south as far as Fernandina, Florida, offering advice and showing medical staff how to prepare herb and root potions to fight disease—dysentery, in particular.

Much to Harriet's relief, she did not have to do all of this alone. Abolitionists in the North rallied people to help with former slaves in the South, and Freedmen's Aid Societies in Boston and Philadelphia began sending teachers and supplies to Beaufort so that people could learn to read and write. Harriet helped these newcomers adjust to the strange, new environment they found themselves in, and she always pumped them for news on the war when they arrived.

In September 1862 Harriet received the wonderful news she had been hoping for. President Lincoln had finally decided that the Union could not win the war without the help of contraband. He intended to proclaim an end to slavery in all Southern states on January 1, 1863. In one hundred days, all the slaves in the South would be legally free! Harriet breathed a huge sigh of relief. At last President Lincoln saw the necessity of "killing the snake," not just wounding it.

The one hundred days sped by, and on New Year's Eve Union gunboats collected thousands of men, women, and children from up and down the rivers near Beaufort. Harriet helped gather wood for a huge bonfire that was being built in a nearby field. As the sun went down, the fire was lit and the celebrations began. Singing and dancing continued throughout the night, and at sunrise the thousands of revelers stood at attention as a band of Union soldiers marched by playing a stirring tune. When the music stopped, everything fell silent. Then there was a drumroll, and a doctor from the hospital stepped up onto a makeshift platform.

"This is a proclamation of the President of the United States," the doctor read from a scroll, "that on the first day of January, in the year of our Lord one thousand eight hundred and sixty-three, all persons held as slaves within any state or designated part of a state, the people whereof shall then be in rebellion against the United States, shall be then thenceforward, and forever free; and the Executive Government of the United States, including the military and naval authority thereof, will recognize and maintain the freedom of such persons, or any of them, in any efforts they may make for their actual freedom."

Not a sound was heard from the crowd after the proclamation was read. In the silence the commander of the First South Carolina Regiment stepped forward to present an American flag to his regiment. The men were all free now, and as freemen they were now officially recognized as soldiers by the government of the United States. Somewhere in the crowd a single voice rose in song.

> My country 'tis of thee,

Other, stronger voices joined in.

> Sweet land of liberty,
> Of thee I sing:
> Land where my fathers died,
> Land of the pilgrims' pride,
> From ev'ry mountain side
> Let freedom ring!

When the song ended, the crowd burst into spontaneous applause. Harriet cheered as loudly as anyone, but before the applause died down, she found herself being hustled up onto the platform. "Say a few words," General Hunter urged her. "The people want to hear from you."

Harriet walked over to the flag that one of the newly freed black soldiers was holding. She took it in her hands and raised her voice. "This is the first flag we have ever seen that promised us anything. This is the first day we have ever had a country," she said.

By "we," she of course meant all her black friends and family, whose freedom she had fought so hard for.

With the Emancipation Proclamation, the Union war effort began to surge ahead. More and more black regiments were established, and General

Hunter began making plans for new military incursions deep into South Carolina. For his plans to take place, he needed the services of someone who was both cunning and courageous. When he looked around for that person, he discovered that only one "man" was good enough for the job—forty-three-year-old Harriet Tubman.

Chapter 14

The Best Man for the Job

We need information. We need to know where rebel troops are stationed, how many there are, how well armed they are, and where they have mined the rivers. You're the person who can get that information for us. Blacks on the plantations throughout the area have heard about you, Moses. They trust you and will hide you and give you the information we need. I want you to be our spy. I know that what I'm asking is dangerous, but you're the best man for the job. If anyone can sneak through enemy lines and collect information, it's you."

Harriet could scarcely believe what General Hunter was saying to her—the best man for the job. Harriet's heart surged with pride. Of course she would accept the assignment!

General Hunter's assessment had been correct. When slaves on the plantations along the rivers learned that she was the Moses who had been working in the Union camp at Beaufort, they gladly sheltered her and gave her detailed information about the numbers and location of Confederate troops in the area. Harriet was able to confirm the rumor they had heard that President Lincoln had indeed set them free and assure them that he was not going to round them up and sell them to new owners in Cuba, as their masters had told them.

Armed with the information Harriet supplied, General Hunter was able to launch many successful raids against rebel army posts along St. Mary's River.

Harriet was so successful in her spying that she was authorized to form a corps of former slaves to serve as spies with her. One of the places her new corps of spies investigated was along the Combahee River, which led inland for about fifty miles from Beaufort. Harriet and her spies were able to learn the location of all the rebel sentry posts along the river and exactly where mines had been laid to sink Union gunboats. With this information in hand, Harriet spoke with her friend Colonel Montgomery, a white man who commanded a regiment of three hundred black soldiers.

"I think we should make a raid up the Combahee," Harriet informed the colonel. "We know where their pickets are posted along the banks, and we know that their main camp is set back in the woods at Green Pond. If we set out at dark, we could be at the railroad bridge at Combahee Ferry by sunup, before the rebs even have a chance to wipe the sleep from their eyes. And we know where they done laid their mines in the river. We can pull those up so the gunboats pass safely."

Colonel Montgomery was impressed by the thoroughness of Harriet's plan, and on the night of June 2, 1863, three gunboats steamed off up the Combahee River. Harriet was at Colonel Montgomery's side throughout the raid, advising and giving orders.

As the gunboats approached the first Confederate sentry post, five Union soldiers went ashore. They crept along the riverbank and subdued the post before the rebel soldiers even had a chance to fire a shot.

The soldiers repeated this at the second and then the third Confederate sentry posts. They moved on upriver in the moonlight, disposing of the rebel mines as they went. After they had overrun the fourth sentry post, more soldiers went ashore. Clad in their dark blue uniforms, they flooded into the plantations along the river. Soon plantation houses, barns, and warehouses were ablaze. The fires lit up the night sky as frightened plantation owners and their families fled inland, while slaves bolted for the river in the hope that they could make it through Union lines to freedom.

Railroad tracks were also torn up and roads blockaded throughout the area. By sunrise the gunboats had reached Combahee Ferry. There they set the railroad bridge ablaze before turning around and heading back downriver. By the time the surprised Confederate troops were able to mount a defense, they were caught in a Union cross fire and retreated.

On the way home, the gunboats began taking aboard the slaves who had fled their plantations. Taking them aboard proved to be a difficult task. When the rowboats arrived at the shore to ferry the slaves to the gunboats, the people flooded into them, overloading them. And fearful of being left behind, those who were unable to get into the boats plunged into the water and held tightly to the gunwales so that the oarsmen could not row.

Seeing the problem, Harriet raised her voice and began to sing.

> Of all the whole creation in the East or in the West,
> The glorious Yankee nation is the greatest and the best.
> Come along! Come along! Don't be alarmed.
> Uncle Sam is rich enough to give you all a farm.

At the end of each verse, the excited freed slaves raised their hands and shouted, "Glory! Glory! Glory!"

"Now!" Harriet shouted, and the oarsmen dug their oars into the water and pushed off from the shore.

Once the freed slaves were aboard the gunboats, the oarsmen rowed back to shore for the next load.

Again Harriet had to lead the freed slaves in a song so that the oarsmen could push off. Slowly the panic subsided and things became more orderly, until all 756 freed slaves had been loaded aboard the gunboats. The people were then transported to a new life of freedom downriver in Beaufort.

The following day General Hunter called Harriet into his office to congratulate her. "That was a splendid military maneuver," he told her. "And it was flawlessly executed—not a single Union soldier was killed or injured. You are to be commended."

Harriet was pleased that everything had gone so well in the only Union raid ever planned and led by a woman.

Soon after the Combahee raid, Harriet dictated a letter to her friend and newspaper owner Franklin Sanborn. She asked Sanborn to send her some things she could not get in the South, including a scandalous new article of women's clothing—a bloomer dress!

> I want, among the rest, a bloomer dress, made of some coarse, strong material to wear on expeditions. In our late expedition up the Combahee River, in coming on board the boat, I was carrying two pigs for a poor sick woman, who had a child to carry, and the order "double quick" was given, and I started to run, stepped on my dress, it being rather long, and fell and tore it almost off, so that when I got on board the boat, there was hardly anything left of it but shreds. I made

> up my mind then I would never wear a long dress on another expedition of the kind, but would have a bloomer as soon as I could get it. So please make this known to the ladies, if you will, for I expect to have use for it very soon, probably before they can get it to me.

Harriet went on in the letter to talk about the campaign on the Combahee.

> You have without doubt seen a full account of the expedition I refer to. Don't you think we colored people are entitled to some of the credit for that exploit, under the lead of the brave Colonel Montgomery? We weakened the rebels somewhat on the Combahee River by taking and bringing away seven hundred and fifty-six head of their most valuable livestock, known up in your region as "contrabands," and this, too, without the loss of a single life on our part, though we had good reason to believe that a number of rebels bit the dust. Of those seven hundred and fifty-six contrabands, nearly or quite all the able-bodied men have joined the colored regiments here.
>
> I have now been absent two years almost, and have just got letters from my friends in Auburn, urging me to come home. My father and mother are old and in feeble health, and need my care and attention. I hope the good

> people there will not allow them to suffer, and I do not believe they will. But I do not see how I am to leave at present the very important work to be done here...

Harriet got her bloomers and continued in her roles as a spy and a scout for the Union army. She could blend in almost anywhere, and she was seldom even noticed by Confederate soldiers. She advised white generals, liberated scores of black slaves, and encouraged everyone to believe that the war would one day be over and they would all live in a free and united America.

Through all of this Harriet was also fighting another battle—one with the War Department itself. The Emancipation Proclamation had set black slaves free, and many of these newly freed slaves signed up as soldiers. However, the War Department would pay black soldiers only seven dollars a month while it paid white soldiers fifteen dollars. This incensed Harriet, who believed that equal work was worth equal pay, regardless of what color the person was. Under Harriet's prodding the black regiments refused to accept any pay until they got as much as their white counterparts. They agreed they would rather fight for free than fight for half their rightful wages. This, of course, meant that Harriet did not receive any pay either, but she felt that the statement she was making to President Lincoln was much more important than money.

A year after the raid up the Combahee River, Harriet realized that she was too exhausted to go on. She needed to rest, and she needed to see how her parents were doing. In June she traveled north. In her pocket was a letter that she had memorized. The letter, from General Hunter, read:

> Pass the bearer, Harriet Tubman, to Beaufort and back to this place, and wherever she wishes to go, and give her free passage at all times, on all Government transports. Harriet was sent to me from Boston by Governor Andrew, of Massachusetts, and is a valuable woman. She has permission, as a servant of the Government, to purchase such provisions from the Commissary as she may need.

This pass was enough to get Harriet back to Boston, where she met another famous black woman, Sojourner Truth. Sojourner told Harriet that she was on her way to see President Lincoln, but Harriet was not interested in joining her on the trip. "Not until he gives black soldiers the same pay as whites," she told her new friend.

When Harriet arrived back at Auburn, she found that her parents were no better or worse than could be expected for a couple in their eighties. More than anything, it seemed they had been worried sick about Harriet.

Harriet settled back into life in Auburn, planting vegetables for her parents and speaking at small gatherings. Many people also came to visit her, including Sarah Bradford, a well-to-do New

York woman who had wanted to meet Harriet for a long time. Sarah wanted to know all about Harriet's adventures and often wrote down the stories Harriet told her.

After a year in Auburn, Harriet felt it was time to get back into action. The spring of 1865 was an exciting time for the Northern states: victory in the war seemed near. General Sherman had marched his troops through Georgia, and upon reaching the coast, he turned north toward Richmond, Virginia. He left a swath of destruction behind him. At the same time, General Ulysses S. Grant and the 125,000 soldiers under his command were hot on the trail of Confederate General Robert E. Lee and his army.

The question for Harriet was, where was she most needed? Was it back in Beaufort, where the war was winding down and everyone was waiting for General Sherman to arrive, or was it somewhere else? She did not know where she should go as she set out for Washington, D.C., in February 1865. However, when Harriet reached Philadelphia en route, a group of women from the Sanitary Commission pressed their need on her. The Sanitary Commission was a volunteer group that had spent the war years trying to improve the terrible conditions in the makeshift hospitals that sprang up to meet the needs of former slaves, many of whom had been wounded in battle.

"You should see the terrible conditions the patients are in," women from the commission told Harriet. "For every soldier who dies on the battlefield, two die in the hospital of disease. There aren't enough bandages to wrap wounds, and amputations are carried out right in the wards, often with small children watching. The smell of rotting flesh is unbearable."

Harriet nodded. She did not need to have the conditions described to her. She had seen them herself in Beaufort and up and down the Atlantic coast. "Where are the worst hospitals?" she asked. "The ones with the highest death rates?"

"Virginia," came the reply. "Smallpox is so bad that we cannot get nurses or orderlies to go and work there. Sometimes the doctors won't go either!"

Harriet sighed. This was not what she had planned. She really did want to be in Beaufort to welcome General Sherman's men, and she had often imagined celebrating the end of the war with her black friends there. But what else could she do? She had asked herself where she was most needed, and here was the answer loud and clear.

Instead of heading back to South Carolina, Harriet Tubman reported for duty at the Colored Hospital at Fortress Monroe in the James River region of Virginia. She took charge of the wards right away, making sure that the floors were scrubbed, the beds deloused, and patients bathed every day. Harriet's whirlwind of activity inspired many other hospital workers, who had almost given up hope, and soon the hospital took on a new air of efficiency.

Harriet continually asked for news of the war, and on April 9, 1865, she was delighted to hear that General Robert E. Lee had surrendered the Confederate army at Appomattox Courthouse. The war was over! But Harriet's work was not. It was time to go to Washington, D.C., to ask that more money be set aside for "colored" hospitals, including the one at Fortress Monroe. She wasted no time in getting to the capital, arriving on April 14, the same night that President Lincoln was shot while attending a performance at Ford's Theatre.

The following day Abraham Lincoln died from his wounds. Celebrations of the end of the war turned to grief and mourning. Harriet thought about the president. Even though Lincoln had been slow to act at the beginning of the war, she had to admit that he was the one who had finally emancipated slaves in the United States. She recalled her conversation with Sojourner Truth and wondered whether she had been right in her assessment of the president. Perhaps Lincoln had been a friend to black people after all.

Despite the gloom that had descended over Washington, Harriet had business to take care of. She made the rounds of various government departments, begging for more doctors, nurses, bandages, and money for her patients.

From Washington Harriet headed back to the hospital at Fortress Monroe, where she planned to stay until the facility was running smoothly. By July Harriet was satisfied she had done all she could for the patients. She was feeling weary, and it was time for her "term of duty" to end. She needed to return to Auburn to rest and look after her parents.

Harriet was exhausted by the time she boarded the train at Washington's Union Station, but she was also full of hope. The war was over, her people were free, and her work was done. She sat down in the nearest empty seat and pulled her War Department pass from her pocket. She knew it said, "War Nurse, Harriet Tubman, Fortress Monroe," and that it entitled her to a half-price ticket back to Auburn, New York.

The train was just gathering steam when the conductor strolled through the carriage selling tickets. His scowl grew as he worked his way back to Harriet's seat. Harriet felt her body tense as he approached. "Don't be nervous," she chided herself. "The war is over. You're not a slave anymore. No one can grab you up and take you away."

Harriet was still trying to relax when the conductor reached her. His eyes were cold as steel. "Come on," he said, kicking Harriet's legs. "Out of here. Black people don't sit on seats on my train!"

Harriet held out the pass she was holding. "I'm a war nurse," she said, "and not only do I have the right to be on this train, I have the right to a half-price ticket, thank you."

The conductor laughed. "Who do you think you are, talking to me that way? You're way too big for your boots. Now you get back to the baggage car where you belong right now."

Harriet stayed exactly where she was, clasping her pass.

"Very well, if that's the way you want it," the conductor said, turning to two men in the seat in front of Harriet. "Come on, men, this darkie is a stubborn one. Help me put her in her place."

Harriet watched as the passenger sitting next to her slid away, giving the men better access to her. The next thing she felt was three sets of hands pulling at her. As she fought back with all her might, the hands got rougher with her. She was dragged into the narrow aisle and kicked and shoved all the way through the door at the end of the carriage. The three men laughed as they pitched her headfirst into the baggage car.

Harriet lay still in the darkness for a long time. The corner of a trunk dug into her back, her shoulder throbbed, and silent tears slid down her cheeks. Harriet had seldom cried in her life—not when she ran away to the pigpen or when the iron weight was thrown at her head. She had not cried when she found her husband had a new wife or when she had helped bury brave black soldiers who had given their lives fighting the war. But now the tears stung her eyes.

Until the moment she was hurled into the baggage car, Harriet had a cause: She was fighting for a better world—a world where black and white people respected each other as human beings. But now, sitting in the darkness of the baggage car, she knew that although the Civil War was over, the battle was not. Instead of resting, she would have to fight on for the dignity of black people and for the rights due them. The struggle should have been over, but it seemed it was just beginning. Harriet's tears kept flowing at the thought.

Chapter 15

Finally Headed Home

All did not go well for Harriet upon her return to Auburn. She was not able to get thoughts of the humiliation on the train out of her mind. The memory haunted her. To make matters worse, a year before the war ended, the War Department had finally agreed to pay black soldiers the same as white soldiers. However, Harriet received no money whatsoever for her efforts during the war. Had she gone back to Beaufort instead of taking up the position at the hospital in Fortress Monroe, she would have received all the pay due her upon arrival in South Carolina, but because she had not reenrolled in the army, she did not qualify for back pay.

With the help of some friends, Harriet gathered all her war papers together and submitted a claim to the government for eighteen hundred dollars, the amount of pay she was entitled to. Her claim soon degenerated into an endless round of pleading, and Harriet began wondering whether she would ever get the money that she had earned.

Worse still, news from the South was discouraging. The new president, Andrew Johnson, seemed to ignore the many awful things that were happening in the former slave states. While he said he did not believe in slavery, neither did he believe in equal rights for black people. Harriet was dismayed to hear that every Southern state was passing laws that discriminated against blacks, almost making them slaves again. These laws, many of which bound illiterate black people to unfair labor contracts, were known as black codes. Race riots erupted in many cities, including New Orleans and Memphis, and a new group of white men with masks over their heads, called the Ku Klux Klan, began terrorizing black people who tried to better themselves.

Thankfully, in 1866 a small group within the Republican Party called Radical Republicans convinced Congress to pass a civil rights act. The Fourteenth Amendment to the U.S. Constitution was also written. President Johnson, a former slaver owner himself, vetoed the act, but Congress had enough votes to override his veto. Harriet learned the fourteenth amendment by heart: "No State shall deprive any person of life, liberty, or property, without due process of law; nor deny to any person within its jurisdiction the equal protection of the laws."

How sweet those words sounded to Harriet! The two measures together ushered in the period in the South known as Reconstruction. For the first time, Southern law made black people truly equal. Blacks voted, some became U.S. senators or representatives, and hundreds of others became local elected officers, such as sheriffs and justices of the peace. But for every victory there were numerous defeats. One of these defeats had to do with Harriet's ex-husband, John Tubman, and it affected her deeply.

In early October 1867, a white man murdered John Tubman. A friend read the newspaper article about the incident to Harriet. The article reported that a man named Robert Vincent had killed John. Apparently the two men had had an argument in the morning, and later that day Robert passed John on the side of the road and pulled out a pistol and shot him dead. John's son by his second wife had watched the whole incident, and there was a witness to the original argument the two men had. The witness was a black woman.

The *Baltimore American* newspaper reprinted a report of the trial from the *Cambridge Intelligence,* an antislavery newspaper. Although the report did not shock Harriet, it saddened her greatly. Following the report the editor wrote a stinging rebuke of the so-called impartial trial of the murderer of the man Harriet had once loved.

> The trial of Robert Vincent for the murder of the colored man John Tubman was

> brought to a close early on Sunday morning last, by the jury rendering a verdict of "not guilty." That Vincent murdered the deceased we presume no one doubts; but as no one but a colored boy saw him commit the deed, it was universally conceded that he would be acquitted, the moment it was ascertained that the jury was composed exclusively of Democrats. The Republicans have taught the Democrats much since 1860...But they haven't got them to the point of convicting a fellow Democrat for killing a Negro.

Such were the problems that faced black people all over the United States. Blacks were now free, but most white people would not accept them as equals. Through it all Harriet toiled on. Her parents continued to need help, especially when her father developed a bad case of rheumatism. Many other needy people arrived at Harriet's door seeking food, clothing, and shelter. Harriet did not turn them away.

Harriet continued her battle to win her back pay and a nurse's pension from the government, but one barrier after another was placed in her way, and the eighteen hundred dollars she was due seemed like a far-off dream.

Others came to her aid, including her New York friend Sarah Bradford. In 1868 Sarah collected stories of Harriet's exploits and testimonials from important political leaders of the day. She put them together into a book called *Scenes in the Life of*

Harriet Tubman. The book sold for one dollar a copy, and the profits went to help Harriet. Eventually Harriet received twelve hundred dollars from the sale of the books. She used much of the money to support two schools for freemen in the South.

The following spring, on March 18, 1869, Harriet surprised everyone, including herself, by marrying a soldier she had met in South Carolina. His name was Nelson Davis, and he was more than twenty years younger than she was. The couple had a large wedding that was attended by many prominent people. Although Nelson was a big man, he was not well. He suffered from tuberculosis. Sometimes he was able to work as a bricklayer, and other times he needed Harriet to take care of him.

While the relationship was an unusual one, it suited them both, and Harriet was happy to have been legally married by a minister. How different this was from her marriage to John Tubman. All those years ago, she and John were not allowed to be officially married under the law, and she had feared that she could be taken from him at any time and sold south.

As time went on, Harriet watched with dismay as Reconstruction began to unravel. Democrats took control of the Southern states one by one. And when they did, their first action was to pass tough new laws against black people. These "Jim Crow" laws were systematically used to keep black and white people separate and to put blacks at a disadvantage. During this time many of the rights abolitionists had fought so hard for were taken away.

Still Harriet did what she could, working with the African Methodist Episcopal Church and speaking out on behalf of black rights.

During the 1870s Ben and Old Rit died. They had both lived to be very old and died free. Others died during this time, too. Harriet's friends Frederick Douglass, Wendell Phillips, and Lydia Child all passed away, and a new generation of black leaders made their way to Auburn to meet the legendary Moses.

Harriet and Nelson Davis spent nineteen good years together until he died in 1888. He was forty-four years old. Upon his death Harriet's brother Henry moved in with her, along with several of her grandnieces and grandnephews.

In 1896 Harriet heard that the twenty-five acres of land and two houses across from her home were up for auction. She had long dreamed of having a bigger place to use as a home for the old and homeless. Although Harriet did not have much money to bid on the property, she went to the auction anyway, hoping for a miracle. She got one. She had the winning bid, and a local bank manager agreed to loan her the money she needed to buy the property.

Harriet moved in, and from then on there were always ten or twelve others living with her. The people of Auburn asked Harriet who it was she wanted to help through opening her home. Her answer was "anyone in need." The place soon became a refuge for both young and old, the sick and the healthy, the blind and the sighted. Harriet loved to garden and cook for her large household and watch the young children running freely over the farmland and the residents helping to grow their own food.

In 1897 Harriet received a surprise parcel from England. The postman read aloud to her the letter that accompanied the package. The letter was from Queen Victoria of Great Britain, who wrote that she had read Sarah Bradford's book and wanted to honor Harriet with her Diamond Jubilee Medal and an invitation to visit her at the palace in London. Harriet was seventy-seven years old by now and thought she was too old for such a long trip, though she appreciated the invitation. The parcel also contained a beautiful black silk shawl, which Harriet placed around her shoulders and seldom took off.

Throughout this time Harriet and her powerful friends continued to fight for the money the U.S. government owed her, but they had no luck. Finally, in 1899 Harriet was awarded a pension of twenty dollars a month, though not for her own war service but because her late husband Nelson Davis had fought in the war and she was entitled to a widow's benefit.

By 1903 the financial strain of paying back the loan on her home became too much for Harriet, and she gave the property to the African Methodist Episcopal Zion Church. The church tried to make the house pay for itself by requiring that everyone who came to stay there had one hundred dollars. This approach greatly upset Harriet, whose entrance requirements had been just the opposite. Since she wanted to help the neediest people who came to her, she would not take anyone in who had money.

Slowly Harriet's energy began to ebb. At first she used a walking stick, and then a wheelchair. But always she had time to tell a story or sing a song. Sometimes she even showed small children an old plantation dance, moving her tired legs up and down as she hummed the tune of a song.

One of Harriet's last public appearances was a trip to church, where she announced, "I am nearing the end of my journey; I can hear them bells a-ringing, I can hear the angels singing, I can see the hosts a-marching, I hear someone say: There is one crown left, and that is for old Aunt Harriet, and she shall not lose her reward."

Finally, in the winter of 1913, Harriet caught pneumonia. By then she was ninety-three years old and felt too weak to get out of bed. Visitors flowed in to see her and listen to her words. On March 10, 1913, she sensed the end was near and asked her friends and family to gather around the bed. As she had done so many times before, Harriet raised her voice and gave an instruction to everyone. "Sing 'Swing Low Sweet Chariot' to me," she said.

The eyes of those in the room brimmed with tears, and the people tried to stifle sobs as they sang softly.

I looked over Jordan and what did I see,
Comin' for to carry me home,
A band of angels comin' after me,
Comin' for to carry me home

As her friends and family sang the final verse, Harriet smiled and breathed her last. Moses had made her final journey.

Many letters were found in Harriet's room after she died. One letter had been refolded so many times that it had almost fallen apart. It was from the great leader of the abolitionist movement, and Harriet's friend, Frederick Douglass. The letter was read by many after her death.

> Most that I have done and suffered in the service of our cause has been in public, and I have received much encouragement at every step of the way. You on the other hand have labored in a private way.... I have had the applause of the crowd and the satisfaction that comes of being approved by the multitude, while most that you have done has been witnessed by a few trembling, scarred, and foot-sore bondmen and women, whom you have led out of the house of bondage, and whose heartfelt "God bless you" has been your only reward. The midnight sky and the silent stars have been the witness of your devotion to freedom and of your heroism.

Outside in the crisp winter air on the night of Harriet's death, the North Star, which had guided her and those she conducted to freedom, shone brightly.

Bibliography

Bradford, Sarah. *Harriet Tubman: The Moses of Her People.* Carol Publishing Group, 1994.

Conrad, Earl. *Harriet Tubman: Negro Soldier and Abolitionist.* International Publishers, 1942.

Conrad, Earl. *Harriet Tubman.* Associated Publishers, 1943.

McMullan, Kate. *Harriet Tubman: Conductor of the Underground Railroad.* Dell Publishing, 1991.

Petry, Ann. *Harriet Tubman: Conductor on the Underground Railroad.* HarperTrophy, 1955.

Sterling, Dorothy. *Freedom Train: The Story of Harriet Tubman.* Scholastic Book Services, 1954.

About the Authors

Janet and Geoff Benge are a husband and wife writing team with more than thirty years of writing experience. Janet is a former elementary school teacher. Geoff holds a degree in history. Originally from New Zealand, the Benges spent ten years serving with Youth With A Mission. They have two daughters, Laura and Shannon, and an adopted son, Lito. They make their home in the Orlando, Florida, area.

Also from Janet and Geoff Benge...

More adventure-filled biographies for ages 10 to 100!

Gladys Aylward: The Adventure of a Lifetime • 978-1-57658-019-6
Nate Saint: On a Wing and a Prayer • 978-1-57658-017-2
Hudson Taylor: Deep in the Heart of China • 978-1-57658-016-5
Amy Carmichael: Rescuer of Precious Gems • 978-1-57658-018-9
Eric Liddell: Something Greater Than Gold • 978-1-57658-137-7
Corrie ten Boom: Keeper of the Angels' Den • 978-1-57658-136-0
William Carey: Obliged to Go • 978-1-57658-147-6
George Müller: Guardian of Bristol's Orphans • 978-1-57658-145-2
Jim Elliot: One Great Purpose • 978-1-57658-146-9
Mary Slessor: Forward into Calabar • 978-1-57658-148-3
David Livingstone: Africa's Trailblazer • 978-1-57658-153-7
Betty Greene: Wings to Serve • 978-1-57658-152-0
Adoniram Judson: Bound for Burma • 978-1-57658-161-2
Cameron Townsend: Good News in Every Language • 978-1-57658-164-3
Jonathan Goforth: An Open Door in China • 978-1-57658-174-2
Lottie Moon: Giving Her All for China • 978-1-57658-188-9
John Williams: Messenger of Peace • 978-1-57658-256-5
William Booth: Soup, Soap, and Salvation • 978-1-57658-258-9
Rowland Bingham: Into Africa's Interior • 978-1-57658-282-4
Ida Scudder: Healing Bodies, Touching Hearts • 978-1-57658-285-5
Wilfred Grenfell: Fisher of Men • 978-1-57658-292-3
Lillian Trasher: The Greatest Wonder in Egypt • 978-1-57658-305-0
Loren Cunningham: Into All the World • 978-1-57658-199-5
Florence Young: Mission Accomplished • 978-1-57658-313-5
Sundar Singh: Footprints Over the Mountains • 978-1-57658-318-0
C.T. Studd: No Retreat • 978-1-57658-288-6
Rachel Saint: A Star in the Jungle • 978-1-57658-337-1
Brother Andrew: God's Secret Agent • 978-1-57658-355-5
Clarence Jones: Mr. Radio • 978-1-57658-343-2
Count Zinzendorf: Firstfruit • 978-1-57658-262-6
John Wesley: The World His Parish • 978-1-57658-382-1
C. S. Lewis: Master Storyteller • 978-1-57658-385-2
David Bussau: Facing the World Head-on • 978-1-57658-415-6
Jacob DeShazer: Forgive Your Enemies • 978-1-57658-475-0

Isobel Kuhn: On the Roof of the World • 978-1-57658-497-2
Elisabeth Elliot: Joyful Surrender • 978-1-57658-513-9
D. L. Moody: Bringing Souls to Christ • 978-1-57658-552-8
Paul Brand: Helping Hands • 978-1-57658-536-8
Dietrich Bonhoeffer: In the Midst of Wickedness • 978-1-57658-713-3
Francis Asbury: Circuit Rider • 978-1-57658-737-9
Samuel Zwemer: The Burden of Arabia • 978-1-57658-738-6
Klaus-Dieter John: Hope in the Land of the Incas • 978-1-57658-826-2
Mildred Cable: Through the Jade Gate • 978-1-57658-886-4
John Flynn: Into the Never Never • 978-1-57658-898-7
Richard Wurmbrand: Love Your Enemies • 978-1-57658-987-8
Charles Mulli: We Are Family • 978-1-57658-894-9
John Newton: Change of Heart • 978-1-57658-909-0
Helen Roseveare: Mama Luka • 978-1-57658-910-6
Norman Grubb: Mission Builder • 978-1-57658-915-1
Albert Schweitzer: Le Grand Docteur • 978-1-57658-961-8
Frederick Douglass: The Right to dignity • 978-1-62486-151-2

Available in paperback, e-book, and audiobook formats.

HEROES OF HISTORY are available in paperback, e-book, and audiobook formats, with more titles coming soon! Curriculum Guides are also available for all U.S. biographies.

www.Heroesofhistory.com